There are good books which are only for adults
but there are no good books which are only for children.

There's something particular about children's books as they can help us to refind things that we do not even know we have lost.

This children's edition of the parable of the Good Samaritan will help you to understand two things. First, that the purpose of your life and your destination is not to follow rules. Rules are needed but not enough to give you what you need. Your destination is to go back where you belong, or better, to be with Whom you are supposed to be with, to create an everyday relationship with Him. And second, that you are members of the strongest and biggest family in human history, that is the Church. And the Church was, is and will always remain not a luxury resort for the chosen ones but a hospital, for the healing of the sickness of human nature and the place where we receive the medicine, Christ, through the sacramental, ascetical and hesychastic Tradition. All of us are sick and the only doctor is Him.

Never forget that He loves you not despite your weaknesses but because of your weaknesses. So, do not listen to all those dream skinners who fill you with guilt by telling you that God abominates you and your mistakes. Not only He does not turn you away, but that is exactly why he came into the world: to meet all those who, while feeling to be a zero, yearn to be His manger.
After all, you will not be judged by who you are, but by who you longed to be.

Good journey!

With Love,

Father Christos

THE GOOD SAMARITAN

A Children's Catechism

THE
Good Samaritan
A CHILDREN'S CATECHISM

V. REV. FR. MICHAEL SHANBOUR

Illustrated by Nicholas Malara

ANCIENT FAITH
PUBLISHING

CHESTERTON, INDIANA

The Good Samaritan: A Children's Catechism
Text ©2019 by V. Rev. Fr. Michael Shanbour
Illustrations ©2019 by Nicholas Malara

Reprinted in
2023 by

ANCIENT FAITH
PUBLISHING

A division of Ancient Faith Ministries
PO Box 748 • Chesterton, IN 46304

store.ancientfaith.com

Library of Congress Control Number: 2022951886

ISBN: 978-1-955890-42-7

PRINTED IN INDIA

This catechism is dedicated to my younger, preteen self,
who could have benefited greatly from it.

– M. S.

TABLE OF CONTENTS

AUTHOR'S PREFACE   *i*

INTRODUCTION
The Good Samaritan   1

LESSON ONE
Paradise: One Big Church   9

LESSON TWO
The Fall: Adam & Eve in Time Out   17

LESSON THREE
The Sickness of Sin: The Darkened Icon   25

LESSON FOUR
Jesus Christ: God's Medicine   33

LESSON FIVE
The Church: Finding the Medicine   39

LESSON SIX

Holy Tradition: The River of Grace   45

LESSON SEVEN

The Priesthood: Guardians of Grace   53

LESSON EIGHT

Holy Communion: The Medicine of Immortality   61

LESSON NINE

Holy Baptism: Born into the Light   69

LESSON TEN

Repentance & Confession: Walking in the Light   77

LESSON ELEVEN

Prayer: Remembering Your Best Friend   83

LESSON TWELVE

Fasting: Praying with Your Body   91

LESSON THIRTEEN

Almsgiving: Praying with Love   99

ENDNOTES   104

AUTHOR'S PREFACE

"OF ALL THE HOLY WORKS, THE EDUCATION OF CHILDREN IS THE MOST HOLY." Implicit in this concise statement of St. Theophan the Recluse is the truth that Christian education is not merely a matter of imparting information but of the very formation of a young person's heart and soul.

By the grace of God, we present this catechism with the hope not only of enlightening our dear children with the unchanging truths revealed to the saints, but as a means of spiritual formation—that the Orthodox Christian Faith might become a living reality in their hearts and lives. We have tried to do so in a way that will engage their imaginative faculty in the most positive sense while maintaining an unbending faithfulness to the Orthodox scriptural–patristic tradition preserved in the experience of the holy Church.

This catechism is the culmination of many years of work and interaction with children (in particular, preteens), both as a youth director and priest, for the purpose of sharing our Faith in a way that is both engaging and understandable for young souls. In that sense, it is truly a labor of love. The specific teachings in this book have been tested successfully in "real time" with the young people of Three Hierarchs Orthodox Church in Wenatchee, Washington. As of the date of this writing, the catechism has also been presented with positive results to other youth by priests, parents, and church schoolteachers.

This work was written with preteen children in mind. Having said this, experience shows that this catechism may also serve as a basic primer for Orthodox Christian teens and adults or even those inquiring into the Faith, as it effectively introduces many of the fundamental truths of Orthodox Christianity necessary for anyone, young or not so young, who desires to know God and His Church.

As a priest, I know that young people are often not a part of the formal catechetical process as families are entering into the bosom of the Church. Adult catechism can simply be too lengthy and incomprehensible for our youth. The wonderful catechetical books available to Orthodox Christians may be "over their heads." Children, and especially teens, are often overlooked or unintentionally neglected in the process. I am painfully aware of the consequences that can occur when young people grow up without a strong intellectual and spiritual connection with the Church's teaching. We hope this catechism helps to fill that void.

The title, *The Good Samaritan*, is inspired by St. John Chrysostom and other Church Fathers who, in addition to the more common moral interpretation of showing Christlike compassion for those in need, have interpreted this parable of the Lord (Luke 10:30–35) as an icon or analogy of the entire economy of salvation. Through this lens we can perceive the Church for what she is—the "spiritual hospital" for the healing of the sickness of sin—and the place where we receive the true "medicine," Jesus Christ, through her sacramental, ascetical, and hesychastic Tradition.

In this catechism we are taken from life in Paradise, through the Fall of Adam and the reality of sin and corruption, and into life and redemption through Jesus Christ. In the Church we then encounter Holy Tradition, the dynamic "river" that runs through the midst of the Church and provides the "living water" for our thirsty souls. The treasure of Holy Tradition then presents to us the Holy Mysteries of the priesthood, the Eucharist, and baptism, along with repentance and Holy Confession, all of which are essential for the health and salvation of our souls. Finally, prayer, fasting, and almsgiving are shown to be the indispensable means of union with God and as lifegiving manifestations of faith, hope, and love. After the introductory chapter, each new lesson begins with a brief summary of the previous chapter.

We have included some supporting informational notes, especially for Lesson One, which describes Paradise and man before sin, as Orthodox Christians are often unaware of the Holy Fathers' harmonious teachings on this important topic. These, however, are contained at the back of the book so as not to clutter the main text. Footnotes that begin with a "T" are teaching footnotes offered to assist teachers or parents by suggesting creative ways of enhancing certain aspects of the lesson. These activity footnotes are placed at the bottom of the pages for quick reference.

When the Holy Scriptures are quoted verbatim, paraphrased, or alluded to the reference is provided in parentheses. However, the use of scriptural citations is by no means complete or comprehensive.

Our book is beautifully illustrated by the gifted Orthodox Christian artist, Nicholas Malara, to visually enrich and reinforce the lessons. We owe him many thanks for his artistic talent, attention to detail, and ardent love for this creative work.

I am thankful for all the extraordinary teachers and examples in my life, who continue to "catechize" me in word and deed. A special heartfelt thanks to my parents, Mitchell and Linda Shanbour, who by their faithfulness introduced me from infancy to the life of the Church; to my loving wife, Makrina, for her support and encouragement; and to my blessed son, Simeon, and the young people of Three Hierarchs Antiochian Orthodox Church, who enthusiastically received these lessons. I am also indebted to my father-in-law, Fr. Joseph Copeland, whose example has been for me an icon of authentic Orthodox Christian life and whose insights, in the words of the holy apostle, have often enlightened "the eyes of my understanding" (Eph. 1:18). If there are any errors in this book, they must be attributed to me alone.

May this work bear fruit for God's Kingdom throughout the years to come!

V. REV. FR. MICHAEL SHANBOUR
October 12, 2022
St. Symeon the New Theologian

The Good Samaritan

Before we start learning about certain teachings of our Holy Orthodox Christian Faith—like "What is baptism?" or "What is prayer?"—we need to understand the *big* picture. The "big picture" means how all the pieces of our Faith fit together to make a whole.

Our Christian Faith is like a puzzle with many pieces.[T1] If we take one piece of a puzzle and look at it by itself, it doesn't tell us much about the entire picture, does it? Even if we take five or six pieces, we can't tell how those pieces fit into the whole puzzle. That's because we still don't know what the picture is supposed to look like. But if we look at the image on the box, we can see what all those little pieces will look like when we fit them together properly.

Our Christian Faith can seem like a puzzle too because there are lots of different pieces. But all of those pieces together make a beautiful picture. It's a picture, or *icon*, of Jesus Christ with His holy Body, the Church.

In order to see the big picture on our spiritual puzzle box, we are going to hear a story that Jesus told us during His earthly ministry. The stories that Jesus told are called *parables*. He told these parables to teach us about God and His Kingdom. This story will help put all the pieces of our Faith

---

T1 Show the children an open puzzle box filled with pieces.
Pick one of the pieces and hold it up.

together to show us what it means to be a Christian—someone who loves God, follows Jesus Christ, lives by the grace of the Holy Spirit, and is a member of the Church.

The story we will hear now is usually called the "Parable of the Good Samaritan," and it is found in the Gospel of St. Luke. This parable will teach us many things. In it we can see all the pieces of our Faith but especially how Jesus Christ saves us from sin and heals us in His Church.

THE PARABLE

LUKE 10:30–35

³⁰A certain *man* went down from Jerusalem to Jericho, and fell among thieves, who stripped him of his clothing, wounded *him*, and departed, leaving *him* half dead. ³¹Now by chance a certain priest came down that road. And when he saw him, he passed by on the other side. ³²Likewise a Levite, when he arrived at the place, came and looked, and passed by on the other side. ³³But a certain Samaritan, as he journeyed, came where he was. And when he saw him, he had compassion. ³⁴So he went to *him* and bandaged his wounds, pouring on oil and wine; and he set him on his own animal, brought him to an inn, and took care of him. ³⁵On the next day, when he departed, he took out two denarii, gave *them* to the innkeeper, and said to him, "Take care of him; and whatever more you spend, when I come again, I will repay you."ᵀ²

T2 After reading the parable once, you may ask children to act it out for a little fun that will help embed it in their memories.

INTERPRETING THE PARABLE

Saint John Chrysostom and other saints of the Church teach us an important way to understand this parable of Jesus. The parable shows us the whole story of God's love for you and me and for all people. Let's look at how the story paints a picture of our Faith.[T3]

A certain man travels.

The man who is traveling is Adam. Do you remember Adam and Eve? They were the first man and woman. They were created by God. They lived in a special place that God created for them called Paradise—a beautiful garden almost like heaven, but on earth. They lived with God, and they were always full of joy. This is the story of Adam, the first man, but it is also your story and my story because we are His children.

The man travels *down* from Jerusalem to Jericho.

Do you know what it's like to travel from Jerusalem to Jericho? You have to go down, down, down. It's like a long hike down from a high hill to a low valley. So, Jesus is telling us that Adam went from a *high* place to a much *lower* place. What is the Lord trying to say to us? He is telling us that Adam sinned. He went from a high spiritual condition, very close to God, down to a low place far from God. By turning away from God through sin, Adam "fell" from a life of happiness and contentment to a place of pain and suffering and death.

The man is attacked by robbers.

What happens to the man as he travels? He is attacked by thieves. The thieves take his robe, beat him, and leave him almost dead. Who are the robbers in our

---

T3 Any of the following statements may be put in the form of a question for children.

story? Here Jesus is speaking about the demons, the devil's fallen angels. The demons desire to rob us of our divine robe, our closeness to God. When Adam listened to the demons and sinned, he lost his spiritual armor, his robe of light. The light is the *grace* of God. Grace is God's very own light and life, which He desires to share with us. We get this robe of light when we are baptized.[T4] But in order to keep it and make it brighter, we have to love and follow God each day, trying not to sin. (If we do sin, we can repent and receive our robe back.) When Adam turned away from God and His light, he was stripped of God's grace, which before had filled his heart and clothed him like a robe. After Adam sinned, he was no longer clothed with God's grace.

The man is left half dead.

Now the story shows us what sin does to us. Sin makes us sick. It hurts us. It brings darkness and spiritual death into our minds and hearts. God created us to be like Him and to have life, to be well. Sin distances us from God and makes us sick or unhealthy. We are not talking about being physically sick, like when our tummy hurts. What we mean is that sin makes our *soul* sick because it separates us from God.

Sin might be compared to eating too much candy; it makes us sick, and we lose all our energy and happiness, and we don't feel well.

The Priest and the Levite pass by the dying man without stopping to helping him.

The Priest and the Levite represent the Old Testament time before Jesus came to heal us. The Old Testament Law was good; it helped people understand the

---

T4 A teacher may display (or put on) a white baptismal robe, explaining that it is given to the newly baptized as a visible sign of the invisible robe of light he receives through baptism.

difference between right and wrong. But it could not fix the sickness of sin and death; it couldn't bring Adam (and all of us) back to life.

The Samaritan comes and stops to help the wounded man.

Who is the "Samaritan"? Do you know? He is Jesus Christ! Jesus is the only one who can really help us, make us well, and bring us back to life with God. Why? Because He *is* God, God's Son, who became human like us so that *we* could become like Him (2 Cor. 8:9; Phil. 2:5–7). He took our sickness upon Himself so it would be possible for us to be healthy again (1 Pet. 2:24). Jesus is the New Adam, the "Second Adam" (1 Cor. 15:47), who brings us back to Paradise, back home to God. He died and rose from the dead to restore us to life with God and cure us of the sickness of sin (1 Cor. 15:17).

The Samaritan pours oil and wine onto the man's wounds.

Oil and wine were used as medicine in Jesus' time. Wine cleanses a wound or sore, and oil helps to heal the wound. By becoming Man, Jesus becomes the medicine to heal us from sin. In the parable, the wine represents the blood that Jesus spilled on the Cross when He died for us to cleanse us from sin. The oil is the lifegiving Spirit that heals and restores our life when Jesus rises from the dead. The oil and wine can also mean Jesus' teachings—His commandments—which cleanse us and heal us.

The Samaritan puts the man on his donkey and takes him to the inn.

The inn was like a hospital. People went there to find rest, to be cured of their sickness, and to be well again. What does the inn represent in the story? The inn is the Church! The Church is the hospital for sinners—you and me. It is the place

5

where Jesus heals us *if* we put our faith in Him and live in Him. It is where God provides the medicine for our sickness of sin. The Church is the place where we can be reborn in baptism (John 3:3–5) so that we are no longer children of Adam, but children of God (John 1:12–13). There, we also receive the "Bread of Life" (John 6:35), Holy Communion, to bring us back to life with God (John 6:51). We also have the Sacrament of Confession to cleanse us when we sin after baptism (1 John 1:9). In the Church, Christ provides us with many other tools and teachings that help us to be healed of sin and receive God's life into our hearts, such as prayer, fasting, and almsgiving (Matt. 6:1–18).

The Samaritan leaves the man with the innkeeper.

Who do you think is the innkeeper? The innkeeper represents the apostles, the bishops, and the priests, who help Jesus heal sinners in the Church. Jesus is the Doctor, and the priest is his assistant. In the Church, God gives grace to the priest so that he is able to heal and lead sinners to God. He gives the Church many forms of medicine that can heal us of sin and unite us to Himself.

As we have mentioned, first God provides Holy Baptism. In baptism we die to sin and are born again to become like Christ, the New Adam (Rom. 6:2–7). We receive again the robe of light that Adam lost in Paradise. Then God gives us the great medicine, Holy Communion, the Body and Blood of His Son, Jesus.

Baptism gives us birth, but it does not make us perfect. How do we continue being healed and growing closer to God, and how are we healed when we sin after our baptism? What medicine do we have? We have the Sacrament of Repentance, when we confess our sins in the presence of the priest, who helps us be forgiven by Christ and healed of our sin.

The Samaritan will come back.

What does it mean that the Samaritan will return to the inn to see how the sick man is doing? It means that Jesus will return to repay everyone for the good or evil they have done (2 Cor. 5:10). Do you remember in the Nicene Creed when we say, "And He will come again to judge the living and the dead"? Christ will come again one day in glory with His holy angels (Matt. 25:31) to put everything into proper order. What a joy that will be for us if we are ready to meet Him!

Now, here is the main point we can take from Jesus' parable: *Everything* in the Church—icons, incense, vestments, the Bible, hymns, prayers, almsgiving, the commandments and doctrines, fasting and struggling against temptation, liturgy and services, sacraments—have only one purpose: to heal us from sin and to join us to God. The Church is heaven on earth. The goal and the purpose of the Church is to make everyone and everything holy and united to God. That is Paradise! The Church is the Paradise that God gave to Adam and Eve. In our next lesson we will learn about Paradise and how Adam and Eve lived with God there.

LESSON ONE
Paradise

In our introduction we painted the "big picture" of how God has rescued us from the sickness of sin. We read the Parable of the Prodigal Son from the Gospel of St. Luke. It tells us the whole story of our lives and God's love for us.

We heard about a certain man who traveled down, down, down from Jerusalem to Jericho. Who does this man represent? He is Adam, the first man, who fell from a life of grace in Paradise down into a world of sin. And what was Paradise? It was the beautiful and blessed place God created for Adam and Eve and their children, to live with Him forever.

But because Adam sinned, his heart was opened up to the "robbers," the demons, who want to rob us of the light of God. Man was left "half dead" because his soul was now sick and deadened by sin. And who saw the poor, half-dead man but didn't stop to help? The Priest and the Levite from the Old Testament time *before* Jesus. They couldn't cure the man because only God could bring him back to health.

And so, God sent the "Good Samaritan." Who is the Good Samaritan? It is Jesus Christ, God's only Son. He became Man to heal us and lift us back up to God. Jesus is both God and Man. It's like God put us on His shoulders so He could raise us back to Paradise.

God created our hearts to reach up to Him, to live in Paradise with Him forever. But sadly, instead of reaching up to God, Adam and Eve looked downward, and they sinned. That left them in a place of sickness and suffering and death. And all of creation suffered too. Animals and plants died now too because of man's sin (Rom. 8:20–22).

ONE "BIG CHURCH"

So, how did Adam and Eve live before they sinned? And where? What was it like? The saints of the Church have given us the answers to these questions, because by God's grace they were made worthy to see Paradise with their spiritual "eyes," and some even visited there.[1]

God created everything from nothing. But before there was something, what was there? Nothing! There was absolutely nothing, except for God, the three divine Persons of the Holy Trinity: God the Father, His Son, and His Spirit. Then when God decided to create the world from His overflowing love, He spoke, and suddenly everything came to be. First light . . . then the sky and outer space . . . the land and the seas . . . grass, plants, and trees . . . sun and moon for the day and the night . . . then birds and fishes, and animals of all kinds. And God saw that everything He made was good (Gen. 1:25). Creation was filled with His goodness, with His light, His life.

Then God created His most marvelous creature—the human being, man and woman (Gen. 1:26). Are you human? (Just checking!) First, He created Adam (Gen. 2:7). He took dust and then breathed into it to make Adam, the first man.

What did He breathe into the dust to make man a living being? The Holy Spirit! We are alive because of the Holy Spirit.[2] If we don't have God's Spirit in us, we are not really and truly alive as God made us!

Just after God created Adam, He put him in a special place of joy, Paradise, in a beautiful garden called Eden (Gen. 2:8). What was Paradise like? It was much more beautiful than any place on earth today.

Listen as I try to describe what Paradise was like.[3]

The ground was likely covered with a beautiful carpet of soft, silky green grass. (Perhaps Adam could take a nap by rolling up the grass like it was a soft mattress or blanket.) The trees were full of delicious fruit all year round; leaves never turned brown, and fruit never rotted.[4]

Adam and Eve were never hungry in the way we are today, with a feeling of emptiness and pain, but when they ate they were filled with joy, and it made them hunger even more for God. Their throats were never dry from thirst, but when they drank it felt like the Holy Spirit was being poured into their bellies. Rivers and lakes were clear and pure like liquid crystal, and there was no pollution.

In the Garden of Paradise, the air was completely pure and sweet,[5] and breathing made one remember the Lord (kind of like church incense does!).

The weather was always beautiful. In Paradise it was never too hot or too cold. There were no tornados or hurricanes or thunderstorms that could scare or hurt any living thing. So, Adam and Eve did not need a house to live in, or even clothing to protect them from the elements.

God gave Adam and Eve dominion and power over everything, even nature. That means they could probably ask the wind to blow harder so they could fly a kite or dry themselves off after a swim. They could ask the sun not to go down until later in the evening so they could finish playing soccer (Josh. 10:12–13).

They didn't wear clothing.[6] Not just because it wasn't cold, but because they had a different kind of clothing. They were wrapped in light: God's own light. Do you remember when Jesus was transfigured on Mount Tabor (Matt. 17:1–8)? Remember how the disciples could hardly look at Him because He was shining with such light? That's the light that covered Adam and Eve.

In Paradise, there was no sickness and no death. Adam and Eve never caught a cold or got the flu. They never broke a leg or bruised a knee. They never got sick, or weak, or old.

Also, before sin, Adam and Eve's bodies were beautiful, light, and strong. In Paradise, they could run forever without getting tired. They could run up a mountain as fast as they could run down. And if they fell, they did not get hurt. There was no pain in Paradise.[7] They did not need to sleep. They didn't have to take naps! But if they did rest, it was a wonderful and peaceful time to spend with God. Their "bed" was God's grace. Their "blanket" was God's love. And their "pillow" was God's peace.

In Paradise the animals were handsome, strong, and gentle. Do you think the animals talked? Adam and Eve were not afraid of them, nor were the animals afraid of Adam and Eve, but they helped them and loved them. The wild bears and lions were man's friends, just as St. Seraphim of Sarov had a wild bear for his friend and a friendly lion dug a grave for St. Mary of Egypt. The saints' holiness allowed them to live as if they were back in Paradise.

Paradise was not just a place *outside* that Adam and Eve could see and touch; it was also how God lived in their hearts. Paradise was also *inside* Adam and Eve because God lived in them and spoke to their hearts. They could hear the voice of God and felt they could almost see and touch Him. They tasted Him when they ate. God gave them the Tree of Life. This Tree was like Holy Communion, and they could have eaten of it eventually if they had remained in Paradise.

God walked in the Garden with Adam and Eve (Gen. 3:8), and they often saw the angels praising God and helping with creation. Maybe they saw their own guardian angels!

In Paradise, prayer poured out of the hearts of Adam and Eve continually like a beautiful song. This is what it means to be healthy as God created us—to have never-ending prayer coming out from our hearts.

But the first man and woman were not completely perfect or grown up yet. God created them in His image, but He wanted them to grow up into His likeness. They were like children, and they still had to learn and grow a lot before they could be even closer to God and become more and more like Him.

God the Holy Trinity—Father, Son, and Holy Spirit—created both man and woman in His image and His likeness (Gen. 1:26). His *image* means that we were made according to the model or mold of His Son (Col. 1:15). It's as if we have an icon of Jesus stamped on our hearts. That icon can never be destroyed, *but* it can be covered over and darkened by sins. His *likeness* means that we can grow to become more and more like God, forever and ever.

This life of spiritual growth in Paradise is how God desired us to live forever. He made us to have great dignity, like good and caring rulers. He made man and woman to be a "king" and "queen" over creation: to take good care of it and to bring God more and more into themselves and into all creation.

Adam and Eve were like priests. They lifted up their hearts in thankfulness to God for all that He gave them, just as the priest and all the people of the Church offer up to God the bread and wine at the Divine Liturgy.

Do you remember in the Divine Liturgy when the priest lifts up his hands and extends an invitation to us? "Let us lift up our hearts! Let us give thanks unto the Lord!" This is an invitation to be like Adam and Eve in Paradise, to do what they failed to do. Did you know that in the Divine Liturgy we experience Paradise for a little while? Do you experience it? Or do you just feel bored and tired?

Paradise—the place where God put Adam and Eve—was like the Church, heaven on earth. But God didn't want Paradise to be a small place, or just for a few people. He wanted us to make the whole world Paradise. He wanted us to help make the whole world a Church—one big Church where people live with God and God with them.

But Adam and Eve only lived in Paradise for a short while. God gave them the ability to make choices. He wanted them to love Him not because they had to, but because they wanted to. He allowed them to make the choice to reject Him and turn away from truth and life. That choice is called sin.

Next we will explain what happened when Adam and Eve sinned. Like the man in the Parable of the Good Samaritan, they went *down* from "Jerusalem" (Paradise) to "Jericho" (sin).

LESSON TWO
The Fall

We have seen that God in His love prepared a special place for man and woman. Paradise was beautiful both outside and in. It was like a big church, where all of God's creation were reminders of Him, of His grace and goodness. It was filled with beautiful plants and fruits and animals, and it also filled Adam and Eve's souls with God's presence and love. You know the feeling right after you receive Holy Communion? This was a constant feeling in Paradise.

God, the Trinity, made everything as an expression of His love. God the Father created everything from nothing, through His Son and His Spirit, in a way that we could experience Him and share the love that the Holy Trinity shares together.

God created Adam's body and soul in His own image—and God's *Image* is Christ. He blew His Spirit into Adam to make him a living being in union with Him. Then He created Eve from Adam's side (Gen. 2:21–22), just as He would one day create His Bride, the Church, from Jesus' side as He hung on the Cross (John 19:34).

God placed Adam and Eve into their specially prepared "palace" called Paradise. If they chose to live with God, they would live there forever—unto ages of ages. They lived with God without pain or sadness, without hunger or thirst, without fear or hatred. They breathed in God's love, and they breathed out prayer and gratitude.

Adam and Eve did not need material clothing because they were clothed with God's Light.[8] They were not naked; they were "robed in majesty" (Ps. 92/93:1)! We could say they were "priests" who offered their whole hearts and lives to God. Isn't this why the priest wears bright and beautiful vestments in the church . . . to express the Light of God?

In this way, we were called to make all creation a Paradise, heaven on earth, one big church!

ADAM & EVE IN "TIME OUT"

When God created Adam and Eve, there was still much for them to learn and to understand about life with God and with each other. They had a long way to go before they were perfected in Him. They were just created, new beings, the first man and woman ever created. They weren't born from a mother like us. Adam was made directly by God. And God made Eve from Adam's rib, from his side. They were "one flesh" (Gen. 2:24)—man and woman, husband and wife.

Everything was new. All they knew was life in Paradise, and life was very good! God took care of them just like your parents take care of you. Adam and Eve were only beginning their life. They were like children. Their bodies were grown up. But they needed to learn and to grow spiritually. Their souls needed to grow up too.

God gave them everything they needed. And He wanted them to love Him and to be obedient so they could always know His embrace. But sometimes kids are not obedient. Have you always been obedient? Tell the truth! Did your mom and dad tell you not to touch a hot plate, but you did, and you burned your hand? Did they tell you not to eat so much candy because you would get sick? Did you eat it anyway and end up with a stomachache? Most of us have done something like that.

Adam and Eve did something like that too. God had given them everything in Paradise for their enjoyment. And He gave them the Garden of Eden with all kinds of plants and trees, full of delicious fruits. The fruit of those trees filled not only their bellies, but their hearts too, with God's love. And you remember, there was also a marvelous tree called the "Tree of Life" (Gen. 2:9). It was the best tree of all! It could make them live forever! If they were obedient to God, they would get to taste of this tree too.

But there was one tree in the middle of the Garden that God told Adam and Eve not to eat from. Do you know what it was called? It was called the "tree of the knowledge of good and evil" (Gen. 2:9). God told them, "If you eat of that one tree, you will die" (Gen. 2:17).

Only one tree! Just one tree they could not eat from! That doesn't sound hard, does it? It's like when Mom says, "You can play over here, or over there, and even *way* over there, but don't go down *there*, close to the river!"

Why does she say that? Is it because she doesn't want you to have fun? No. It's because she doesn't want you to get hurt, right? It's not a bad thing to be close to the water, is it? Water is a good thing. It quenches our thirst and keeps us alive. But if we're young, and we don't yet know how to swim well, we could fall into the river and drown.

But sometimes we're tempted to do it anyway, aren't we? Maybe bad thoughts come into our heads: "Mom never lets me do what I want!" or "Mom just doesn't want me to have fun!" Or maybe a friend says, "You won't get hurt. Moms just don't understand."

This is what happened to Adam and Eve. But it wasn't a friend who tempted them. Who was it? It was a snake—the devil—in the form of a serpent. The serpent said to Eve: "Did God tell you that if you eat of that tree you will die? You won't die! God is limiting you. He knows that if you eat the fruit from this tree, you will know everything like He knows everything. You will be as powerful as Him. You will be like gods on your own, *without* God" (Gen. 3:4–5).

What did Eve do? She listened to the serpent. And she began to think, "Such beautiful fruit can't be *that* bad. It looks really delicious, and I will be smart and will be able to do grown-up things." Eve was tempted with pride. And so, she ate (Gen. 3:6).

Then she gave some to her husband, Adam. And he ate too. And what happened? They began to feel different inside: sad and lonely and cold. God seemed so far away now. Things changed outside too.

Remember how Adam and Eve didn't need clothing? Now they were no longer clothed with God's light. The light coming from their hearts faded away, and they realized they were naked (Gen. 3:7). So, Adam and Eve were embarrassed and afraid, and they tried to hide from God. Is it possible for us to hide from God? Is there some place we can go where God cannot see us? No! God sees and knows everything.

God saw what Adam and Eve did. What did God do? Did He stop loving them? No. He hoped they would be sorry and repent. He hoped they would take responsibility for their actions.

Do you know what it means to "take responsibility"? It means to be honest, to own up to what we do and not to blame someone or something else. So, if we're playing outside and we break our neighbor's window, what should we do? We should go and tell the truth and then ask how we can help to make things better.

God asked, "Adam, why are you hiding? Did you eat of the tree?" But Adam didn't confess his sin or ask God to forgive him. What did he do? He blamed his sin on his wife, Eve. He even blamed God for making her his wife! (Gen. 3:12).

Then God asked Eve, "Did you eat of the tree I asked you not to?" But Eve didn't take the blame for what she did either. She blamed it on the serpent (Gen. 3:13).

God wanted to give Adam and Eve a chance for confession. But they didn't confess their own sin; they confessed the sin of others. In the Church, God has given us the Sacrament of Confession. Have you been to confession? We stand before the icon of Jesus, with our priest, God's assistant. And whose sins do we confess? Only our own, right? We don't blame others like Adam and Eve did. This is very important to keep us healthy and close to God.

God was very sad that Adam and Eve were disobedient to Him and that they believed the serpent instead of His Word. Now they could no longer live in Paradise. They brought sin into themselves and into the world. And sin is like a poison that makes us sick. God would have to take them out of Paradise, and they would eventually die because they had separated themselves spiritually from God.

God still loved them—He loves us all! But Adam and Eve had made themselves sick with sin. They were sick, and they couldn't enjoy Paradise anymore. They could not live close to God for now. God had to put them in "time out" until He could do something to cure them. Adam and Eve needed very strong medicine to bring them back to true life.

It wouldn't be forever. God had a plan to make them well again. He would give them the medicine that would make them healthy and alive again. The medicine is Jesus. And the hospital is the Church. God would send the medicine when the time was right.

In the meantime, He told Adam and Eve what they could expect now while living in a world of sin. To the woman He said, "You will give birth to your children in great pain" (Gen. 3:16). Then He said to the man, "You will have to work hard to cultivate the land in order to grow your food" (Gen. 3:17). Life would be hard. There would be pain and sadness, sickness and death. God created clothes from animal skins to cover their naked bodies (Gen. 3:21). And He sent them out of Paradise. God put an angel to guard the door to Paradise so that they wouldn't eat of the Tree of Life and live forever in sin (Gen. 3:22–24). God did all of this out of *love*.[T5]

[T5] You may read the story of Adam and Eve's sin from Genesis, chapter 3, as the children act it out.

The Sickness of Sin

In the last lesson we learned what led to a "time out" for the first man and woman, our ancestors: Adam and Eve. What happened and why did God have to put them in time out?

He had created them with the ability to live forever in communion and enjoyment with Him. They were like children who had the choice of how they would grow up—into perfection with God in obedience to Him or by going their own way. God had given them only one rule: "Please don't eat of that tree because it will make you sick, and you will die. That tree is life without Me" (Gen. 2:17).

What did our ancestors do? They were tempted by the devil. He lied to them. He always lies. He told them, "God does not want you to eat of that tree because He knows it will allow you to grow up and make your own decisions. You will be an adult now and do whatever you want. It will make you like God" (Gen. 3:4). And the fruit of that tree looked really delicious!

But when they ate, something terrible happened. Their lives changed for the worse. They didn't become like God; they became sick with sin. Sin separates us from God. Adam and Eve lost their beautiful robes of light, and they entered a life of pain and suffering. God gave them a chance to tell the truth about what they did, but instead of confessing, they blamed one another. They blamed God's creation.

God took them out of Paradise for a "time out." He would wait for the right time to send the Medicine to make them well again and bring them back to life.

THE "DARKENED ICON"

God saw that Adam and Eve had made themselves sick with sin. And because He loved them, He sent them out of Paradise so they would not live forever in sickness, sadness, and pain. Because their souls were now sick, their bodies would also eventually die. But God did not create Adam and Eve to die. He did not create death! He was sad to see their hearts darkened and sick with sin. For this meant their hearts could no longer see Him and experience His perfect love.

Because we are children of Adam and Eve we also live with this sickness. What is this sickness of sin? And how can we become healthy again?

We have already learned that God created us in His own image, with His own stamp. Have you ever gotten a stamp on your hand? What kind of image or picture did the stamp make?

What do you think *God's* stamp is? God's stamp is Jesus Christ. Jesus is God's image, His icon (Col. 1:15). He made Adam and Eve, and every person ever born, with the stamp or icon of Jesus in his or her heart. Did you know you have the icon of Jesus in your heart?

God created Adam and Eve with a beautiful icon of Christ stamped on each of their hearts. [T6]

But when Adam sinned, the icon became dark and dirty. The icon was covered over by sins, like mud or dust covers over a window or a beautiful picture.[T7]

Imagine a bright and beautiful icon of Jesus Christ. Now imagine that the same icon has been buried in the ground for many years. What has happened to the icon? It has become dark and dingy, dirty and dim. Can you see the image well now? No! It needs to be cleaned. This is what happened to Adam and what happens to us because of sin.

Now, after Adam sinned he had difficulty seeing the stamp of Jesus in his heart. This means that Adam forgot about God and thought mostly about himself and his own desires. He no longer sensed that God was in him and with him. Do you ever forget about God?

Before he sinned, Adam never forgot about God, whether he was walking, or eating, or enjoying the creation, or even sleeping. What causes us to forget our Creator? The sickness of sin causes us to forget—or even to ignore—God. Our forgetfulness of God is a sign of our spiritual sickness—the sickness that came into the world when Adam and Eve sinned.

T6 A parent or teacher may now place an icon of Christ over their heart.

T7 Before the lesson, use wax paper and a marker to draw the outline of a heart along with the names of a number of sins (pride, envy, anger, unkindness, lack of faith in God, gluttony, greed, selfishness, stubbornness, etc.) in and around the heart in various sizes and directions. You may also darken the areas in between and around the words. Now place the wax paper drawing over an icon of Jesus Christ.

Who could clean the darkened icon in man's heart? Who could restore or clean up the perfect picture of Christ in us? Who could make man's heart healthy again? Could Adam? Eve? Could the Holy Prophet Moses or even St. John the Baptist? No! No one but Jesus Christ Himself could do this. (We'll learn about this in the next lesson).

How else was Adam sick with sin?

God made man's heart so that he could see Him and see angels and see all of creation as God's gift and blessing. God created us with spiritual "eyes." This is a kind of eyesight that can see or understand things that are normally invisible to our physical eyes (Eph. 1:18). Our Church Fathers call this "the eye of the soul." In the Greek language the eye of the soul is called the *nous*. Do you have a nous? Maybe no one ever told you before, but you *do* have a nous!

Your nous is deep in your heart where God's image is. If your nous is clear and clean, you can sense God in everything, just as when your physical eyes are open and work well, you can see everything around you. But if your nous is darkened by evil thoughts and sins, you are like someone who walks with his eyes closed, or who forgets to turn on the light at nighttime.

When our nous is healthy and good, we keep our spiritual eyes on God, we remember Him, we can feel Him and hear Him. Have you ever looked through a window at nighttime? What do you see? Darkness, right? When our nous is dark—when the light of God is not in us because of sin—we can't see God clearly (Matt. 6:22–23).

When Adam sinned, his nous, the "eye of his soul," was darkened. Now he felt as if God was no longer with him—that He was far, far away. Was God far away? No! God was not far away. But because of sin, Adam was trying to find God through a dark window, through his darkened nous.

Not being able to see God with the eye of his soul made Adam spiritually sick. Instead of loving God he began to love *things* he could touch with his hands, hear with his ears, see with his eyes, taste with his mouth, and even smell. Those things are not bad, but Adam tried to *replace* God with those things, things that made him feel good for a short time. God created the things of the world to help us remember Him and love Him, not to replace Him! But now Adam used the things of the world to try to make himself happy without God.

Are we happy without God? Hmmm . . . some people try to be!

What kinds of things do people use to make themselves happy without God? Money, food, other people, things they buy, and much more!

When Adam's spiritual eye was darkened, he developed what we call "passions." And all of us who were born of Adam also have passions. What are passions? Passions are strong desires that turn us away from God and His goodness. They tempt us to think or do evil, or to lose faith in God, or to hate or hurt others who are made in God's image.

Do you know the names of any of the passions? Anger, hatred, selfishness, jealousy, fear, lying, hopelessness, greed, pride, etc. Have you ever felt any of the passions? Are you sure?

The passions are like magnets that have attached themselves to our hearts. Our passions are attracted to sin, like one magnet is attracted to another.[T8]

Like a magnet, when our passions get too close to sin, they want to stick to it. These passions pull us toward sin. And the more we sin, the stronger the magnetic force becomes. Sometimes it feels like we can't stop from sinning, but with God's grace we can.

Everyone has passions, even the saints. But the saints fought hard to keep the passions out of their hearts. They didn't let the passions control them (Gal. 5:24).

T8 Demonstrate this by placing one magnet on your heart. Bring another magnet, with the opposite pole facing you, closer and closer. Soon a magnetic force will cause them to attract and stick to each other.

We can follow the way of the saints too. The more they resisted sin, the more their magnets (passions) lost power to pull them into sin. Their passions found a different direction—they turned their passions over, away from sin and toward God.[T9] Then they were free to move toward God. They were no longer slaves to sin (Rom. 6:6), but servants of God (Rom. 6:22).

In the same way, when we continually turn our hearts to God, we are no longer pulled toward sin. Sin no longer sticks to us.

The saints cleaned their hearts from the dark passions so that the light of God could come in. When the light of God comes into our hearts, we can see what is really important and true. Our spiritual eye—our *nous*—is filled with light. We find joy and peace. Then we can turn our attention to the love of God and our neighbor.

It's hard to keep our attention on God, isn't it? We get distracted. Do you know what it means to be distracted? It's when we try to focus on something, but something else grabs our attention. Does that ever happen to you? How about when you're in church? When you pray, do you ever get distracted and begin thinking about something else? It happens to most of us! Do you know why? Because our attention, our nous, is distracted; we are distracted from God. We begin thinking about something we really want, and we forget about God. We are disturbed or become afraid, and we lose faith in God. This is part of the sickness of sin.

Remember when the disciples were in the ship and Jesus was down below sleeping? A storm came, and the winds were fierce, and the waves tossed the boat around. The disciples became afraid and lost their faith, even though Jesus was right there with them (Matt. 8:23–27).

T9 Turn one of the magnets over, and you will find that the two magnets will no longer stick to each other, no matter how hard you try. Instead, they push away from one another.

So, now we know what it means to be sick with sin:

The icon, or image, of God in us becomes dark and dirty.

The eye of our soul, our nous, is darkened and no longer sees God
or hears His voice clearly.

We become filled with the passions, the "magnets"
that try to pull us toward sin.

And worst of all, sin and death come to live
in our souls and bodies.[9]

Next, we will learn how God's Son, Jesus Christ, provides the medicine to save us from all this and make us well again.

LESSON FOUR

Jesus Christ

We have learned how sin made us spiritually sick. It covered over the image of God in us. It darkened our spiritual eyes, so we could no longer see God and live with Him. It filled our hearts with passions that pull us like a magnet away from God and toward sin. And if that were not enough, death came to separate us from God.

With our spiritual eyes unable to see God and our natural energies turned away from God, human beings became distracted by the things of this world. We began to desire things more than God, thinking that they would make us feel good. But it didn't work. And it never works. At least not for long!

This is the human sickness of sin. To overcome sin, we had to be turned in a new direction. But who could turn all of humanity in a different direction?

GOD'S MEDICINE

Human beings were in trouble—wouldn't you agree? We needed medicine, not just for our bodies, but for our souls. We needed the light to be brought back

33

to our spiritual eyes. We needed to be reborn and remade to get the sin out and get God's grace back in. And we needed someone who was stronger than death. Like the man in the Parable of the Good Samaritan, we needed someone to have *compassion* on us, to stop as we lay on the road wounded and half dead, and bring us back to life.

Who could do all this? Who could make our human nature healthy and alive again? Was there anyone who could take upon himself the sin that makes us sick? How about the sin of the whole world? And who could rescue us from death, since death had swallowed up everyone who had ever been born? Who was stronger than death?!

You may know the answer already. It is the Good Samaritan: Jesus Christ. God the Father sent His Son to become the medicine that can make us well. "For God so loved the world that He gave His only begotten Son, that whoever believes in Him should not perish but have everlasting life" (John 3:16).

But how did Jesus become the medicine we needed?

First, He clothed Himself with our human nature—He became Man. Because of Adam, the first man, our human nature became sick with sin. But now, Jesus Christ, the New Adam *who had no sin*, would reverse what old Adam did by putting on our human nature and making it healthy once again. He did something even greater—He joined our nature with God!

Have you ever put your shirt on inside out? It looks kind of funny, right? The picture on the shirt isn't very clear, and the tag is sticking out. That's how our human nature had become because of sin. So how do you fix the shirt that's inside out? You pull it off to make it right side up and put it back on. That's sort of what God did for us.[T10]

God's Son, Jesus, put on our inside-out humanity and made it right side up by

---

T10   This may be displayed, keeping modesty in mind.

living a sinless life in perfect communion with God the Father. Jesus' humanity was right side up, so the image of God in Him was not fuzzy, but perfectly clear. His nous, His spiritual eye, was full of light. And His humanity didn't have any of our sinful passions. There were no "magnets" to pull Him away from God His Father.

Jesus made our human nature alive again by joining it to God's nature, taking all the sickness out. He remade us by putting on what we're made of.

And now each of us can be remade by putting *Him* on. That's what happens when we are baptized. We put on Jesus Christ and His clean and healthy humanity: "As many of you as were baptized into Christ have put on Christ" (Gal. 3:27).

But Jesus remaking our humanity is only *one* part of the medicine.

Jesus not only became Man to heal our sick nature, He also took our sins upon Himself on the Cross (1 Pet. 2:24). Jesus is the medicine for our sins too. When Jesus allowed Himself to die on the Cross, He absorbed Adam's sin and the sins of the whole world—past, present, and future.

Have you seen how a large sponge can absorb water? Place the sponge into a bowl of water, and the water is taken up completely into that sponge.[T11] It disappears! Then you can take the same sponge and squeeze the water back out into the earth or down the drain.

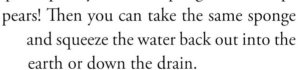

This is something like what our Lord Jesus did on the Cross. He absorbed our sins like a sponge into His pure and sinless body and soul because of His love for us. He was the only One who could soak up our sins because He alone is without sin. And He alone is not only Man, but God. As God, He is bigger than all of heaven.

T11   You may wish to show the children how this works.

All of our sins are like a tiny drop for Him. He then drained all of that sin—*our sin*—out of His humanity and into the sea of His love so that we could be free from sin if we live in Him.

The devil would laugh every time a human being died, even righteous people like Abraham, Isaac, and Jacob. Because even though they were righteous and loved God, death still reigned because of sin (Rom. 5:14). They could not escape death, which came from sin. Death had become the devil's weapon to keep man in his grasp, imprisoned by sin.

But what about Jesus? He was not just Man but also God. Adam was not His father; *God* is His Father. And His mother is Mary, the Most Holy Theotokos. He had no sin, so the devil had no power to keep Him in death. Still, the devil thought if he could get men to kill Jesus, he would win. What he didn't know is that even death, the strongest thing in this world, was not strong enough to hold Christ our God. When Jesus, the Second Adam, accepted death on the Cross for us, He broke the power of sin for all of us children of the first Adam.

When Jesus died and His soul went into Hades (Eph. 4:9), the place of death, He met the devil face to face. And, oh, was Satan afraid! The devil was afraid and cried out because he could not find any sin by which to hold Jesus. He realized Jesus was stronger than death, but it was too late!

Now, death is the result of sin (Rom. 6:23). So, by His sinless death on the Cross, Jesus destroyed the power of sin, the only power the devil had (Heb. 2:14–15).

Yet Jesus' work was not done. There was one more thing to do to bring us back to God the Father. What happened after Jesus died and was buried in a new Tomb? He rose again on the third day, Sunday. Christ is risen!

When we say Christ rose from the dead, we don't just mean that He came back to life like you and I are living right now. He didn't rise from the dead like He raised Lazarus, because Lazarus still died again when he got older. When Jesus rose from the dead, there was no death in His body. It's not just that He was breathing again. Jesus was raised to a new kind of life, the life of *Resurrection*.

It is a life where sin and death have no power. And it is *eternal life* (Rom. 6:23): it lasts forever and ever, and ever and ever, unto ages of ages. Amen!

Also, resurrected life means that Jesus' body and soul were filled with God, filled with God's life, His light. Jesus' resurrected body was like Adam and Eve's body before they sinned—no sickness, no sorrow, no need for food or drink or sleep. It is even *more* than that because Adam and Eve *could* die. But because of the Resurrection, Jesus could never die again (Rom. 6:9). In fact, Jesus took His resurrected body to heaven to the right hand of God, the Father (Luke 24:51; Acts 1:9). And He has prepared a place there for us as well (John 14:2).

After Jesus rose from the dead and ascended into heaven, He sent the Holy Spirit on the day of Pentecost so that our souls and bodies can receive God's life and light as well. He became the best and most powerful medicine for us. Medicine stronger than death! Medicine that joins us to God forever. We still die, but Jesus "trampled down death by death" and made death to be the doorway to eternal life. He poured out the power of death and filled it up with life (John 11:25).

Have you ever come to a door and didn't know what was behind it? When you opened it, were you surprised? Did you expect to see what you saw? Well, if we have God's life in us, if we have joined ourselves to Christ, then our death will be like a door that opens up to a life we never imagined: a life of joy, perfect love, and no more death.

This is the good news, the *gospel*—that Christ is risen! Jesus has become our medicine. He remade us by becoming Man, He destroyed the power of sin and death through the Cross, and He rose from the dead to take away our sickness and fill us with His life!

The Church

We've learned how Jesus became our medicine by taking our sins upon Himself, destroying death, and rising from the dead to give us eternal life. This is the Good News, the gospel: that God sent His Son to become the medicine, so that believing in Him, we can be healed of our sin, be united to God, and overcome death by the Resurrection.

What was God's "recipe" for the medicine that we needed?

First, He had to send His Son, who is God, to become Man. Jesus is the God-Man. He was always God! But from the time He was in Mary's womb, He also became Man, like us, but without sin. So, He is *fully God* and *fully Man*! Jesus, the Son of God, our Savior, is *one* Person in *two* natures. He united our human nature with His divine nature. This is how God healed our human nature.

Jesus also overcame the power of sin by dying on the Cross as Man. Like a sponge absorbs water, Jesus absorbed the sin of the world when He allowed Himself to die. Afterward, He squeezed that sponge, and all the sin, our sin, came pouring out, down into the drain of His love and forgiveness. This is how He healed our sin.

Then Christ Jesus rose from the dead, "trampling down death by death." He swallowed up death with life (1 Cor. 15:54)! He beat the devil at his own game! God planned a surprise attack. The devil thought he had a mere man, but instead he found himself face to face with God! And now, for all who are united to Jesus, death will be a doorway to life with God.

This is our medicine.

FINDING THE MEDICINE

But how do we get this medicine?

From now on, in our catechism we will be talking about where we can find God's medicine and how to get it. First, let's learn about *where* we find our medicine: Jesus Christ.

Remember the times you've been sick or hurt, and you needed help to be healed? Maybe you broke a bone or sprained your ankle. Perhaps you had an infection or a bad fever. Maybe you burned your skin. Some kids have asthma attacks and have trouble breathing. You may have cut yourself or slipped and hit your head. Other times, you didn't even know why you felt bad!

Where did your parents take you? They took you to the hospital or a special medical clinic. Those in charge looked you over to figure out what was wrong. They asked you what happened and where your pain was. Then they decided the best treatment and how to bring you back to health: they put your bone back into alignment; they stitched up a deep cut; they applied cream to your burn; they gave you medicine and told you to rest.

The hospital provided the right treatment and medicine for you. At the hospital, the doctor is in charge. He is the head. The doctor gives orders to his trusted helpers to provide the medicine and to comfort the patient. In this way, our bodies can be healed.

So, where do we get the *spiritual* medicine that the Lord Jesus has for us by His becoming Man, dying, and rising again?

It is similar to the doctor and the hospital. Jesus is the doctor, the Great Physician, and the Church is the hospital. It is in the Church that we find the medicines for our soul. The medicine is from Christ, who is the Head, but we find it in the Church, His Body.

And who are the Lord's trusted helpers to whom He has given orders for our healing? Who is it that gives us the right kinds of medicines to heal us? If you said "the bishop" or "the priest," you're right!

Remember the Parable of the Good Samaritan? We know that Jesus is the Good Samaritan. Only Jesus could help the man who had been hurt by the demons. But where did He take the man? He took him to the inn—the Church, the spiritual hospital. And He gave him over to the innkeeper, right? Who is the innkeeper? The bishop or priest! So, Jesus brings all of us who are spiritually sick in various ways to the Church, and He asks the bishops and priests to assist Him in healing us.

The Church is the place where we find the medicine to heal our spiritual wounds, our sinfulness, to make us whole and to unite us with God. The purpose of the Church is to heal our sin. The whole life of the Church is an assortment of spiritual medicines that can heal our soul and body.

Having received his orders from Christ, and using the medicine cabinet of the Church, the priest seeks to stitch up the deep cut of anger, to calm the burning of evil desires, to restore our faith and help us breathe deeply again, to correct our thoughts, and, with the doctrines of Christ and His Church, to put our "bones" back into alignment and strengthen us to stand firm against the temptations of the world. He prescribes medicines to bring us back into a loving relationship with God and with our neighbor.

But the medicine is not a pill or a cream; the medicine is God's own life, the Holy Spirit. If we open our hearts, God pours His own life into us (Rom. 5:5). This medicine is even "better than life" (Ps. 62/63:4); it is eternal life—perfect love that never ends (1 Cor. 13:8). It is the kind of life that raised Jesus from the dead. It is the life that cannot be overpowered by death.

Now, there is a specific name we use for this life of God that has become our medicine. Do you know what it is called? The Church calls it God's "grace." Grace is the life of God that is poured out by the Holy Spirit in the Church and into the hearts of His people.

Grace is not something that God *makes*. No, it is His own life, the life that flows from God Himself. Grace is also called God's "power" and His "energies."

Once when Jesus was on His way to heal the ruler's daughter, the people crowded all around Him (Mark 5:21–24; Luke 8:40–42). A sick woman came up behind Him and touched Jesus' robe. We know her as St. Veronica. What happened? She was healed of her sickness! Even though there were many people around Jesus, pressing against Him, Jesus knew that St. Veronica had touched Him. How did He know? Because Jesus felt "power" going out from Him (Luke 8:46; see also Luke 6:19). That power is the grace of God.

Here is another example from the Bible:

The book of the Acts of the Apostles tells us that people used to bring handkerchiefs and aprons and place them on St. Paul's body (Acts 19:12). Then they took these and touched them to the bodies of sick people. In this way the sick were healed! How could a piece of cloth heal people? Because it was filled with God's grace, God's power and life, from touching St. Paul, whose soul and body were filled with God's grace.

God's grace is found in His Church and in the faithful members of His Church. But how is it that God's grace is in the Church? Because Jesus is joined to His Church as a head is joined to a body. The Church is so close to Him that Christ is called the "Head" and the Church is called His "Body" (Col. 1:18). Does your head go anywhere without your body? I hope not! Does your head take a vacation from your body? Of course not! Your head is attached to your body. It is *one* with your body.

The same is true with Christ's Body. Christ and the Church are *one*. The Church is always connected to Him. We can even say that the Church *is* Jesus Christ, because St. Paul says that the Church is Jesus' Body. Jesus, the "Head," is always united to His Body. We have to be careful, though. Some members of the Church can separate themselves from Christ's Body through their sins. But the life of Jesus can always be found if we are truly joined to Christ in His Church.

Now, just as there are different kinds of medicines for different kinds of sicknesses, God's grace is also given to us in the Church in different ways. Since the Church is Christ's Body, all the holy prayers and actions of the Church are mysteries that bring God's grace and life to us.

In the next lesson, we will learn about all these medicines that are available to us in the Church. Together, they are called "Holy Tradition."

LESSON SIX
Holy Tradition

In our last lesson, we learned that God heals us in the Church. The Church, the *Body of Christ*, has the medicine to heal all people and bring them back into God's warm embrace. You know what an embrace is, don't you? It's a big hug. God wants to hug us. When Jesus spread out His arms on the Cross God showed His love for us, that He wants to embrace us forever. And He wants to make us well and free from sin so that we can hug Him back!

Jesus Christ is the Doctor, the Healer. And the Church is the Hospital, the place where we can find the medicine for our souls and bodies. The priest is called to be Christ's "mouth" and His "hands" by which we receive the medicine for our healing and growth. With his mouth the priest is to teach us God's Word. With his hands the priest gives us new birth through baptism, seals us with God's Spirit, covers us with God's forgiveness, and feeds us with Christ's Body and Blood in Holy Communion.

And what is this medicine that God offers to heal us and lead us back to Himself? What is it called? It is called His divine *grace*. Grace is God's own presence—His life. We also call it His power, His energies, and His love for us. It is not a created thing, but God's *uncreated* power. God is uncreated, and His grace is uncreated.

45

The grace of God fills us with God Himself. He wants us to drink as much of this medicine as we can. He wants us to drink of His abundant and ever-flowing grace like we might drink from a beautiful, pure, and refreshing river.

THE RIVER OF GRACE

Now, did you know there is a river that runs through the Church? There is a river of grace! It is what keeps the medicine flowing to all who need it. What is this river of grace? It is called the Tradition of the Church—Holy, or Sacred *Tradition* (1 Cor. 11:2; 2 Thess. 2:15; 3:6).

The Holy Tradition flows from God the Father, through His Son, and by the Holy Spirit into the Church. It is a river that flows from God—it was not made by men, but comes from God Himself.

Holy Tradition is not just a set of ideas that really smart people made up one day, or even over many centuries. It is the way of living that brings the healing grace of God into our souls. It is the way of life that God has shown opens our hearts to Him and joins us to Him.

God has shown this "Way" (Acts 9:2)—Holy Tradition—to His saints. And we, His people, follow the way of His saints. Why? Because the saints (sometimes we call them the Holy Fathers or Mothers) have proven that this is the way to God. How have they proved this? By their lives—the way they believed, lived, and worshipped. And by the results. They became holy, like God Himself. The Bible tells us to imitate their faith (1 Cor. 4:16; 11:1; 2 Tim. 3:10; Heb. 6:12). We are called to follow them as they followed Christ (Heb. 13:7).

We are Christ's disciples, but we are also the disciples of the saints who show us the way of Christ. They pass down the Holy Tradition of the Faith of Christ by their way of life and sometimes through their teachings. The saints are icons of Christ and Holy Tradition.

The most holy saint of all is Mary, Theotokos. She is called in Greek *Panagia*, "All-Holy." She is the most perfect example of obedience to God. Without her obedience we would not have our Savior, Jesus Christ. She gave her whole self to God, before, during, and after giving birth to Christ our God. We follow her humble and holy way because, as the Angel Gabriel said, she is "full of grace" (Luke 1:28).

Holy Tradition means everything that Jesus Christ taught His apostles and how the Holy Spirit guides the Church to keep His teaching true, fresh, and alive. It means how the saints and teachers of the Church have kept the Faith and have shown us how to keep the Faith.

Have you ever seen a treasure map? It's a map that shows you how to find a valuable treasure like money, or gold, or precious jewels. It shows you how to get from where you are now to where you want to go as quickly as possible. Without a map you might never find the treasure. Or you might turn the wrong direction and fall off a high cliff. The Tradition of the Church is like a treasure map. It shows us how to get from a place of sin to becoming holy, like God. It shows us the path that the saints walked to be united to Jesus Christ, who is the greatest treasure of all. And it tells us where the dangers are, so we don't turn the wrong way and hurt ourselves spiritually.

Tradition is our map to God. And how did we get this map? It is not from the minds of men, but from the mind of God. God revealed it through Jesus, and Jesus handed it down to His apostles (John 17:6). And with the help of the Holy Spirit, the apostles handed it down to those who came after them, especially those who were selected to be bishops (2 Tim. 2:2). And those bishops handed it down to the next bishops and all their people, and the next bishops to the bishops after them and to their flocks . . . and on and on until it gets to us today.

This is how the river of grace flows down to us. It keeps being passed down so we also can drink from the waters of Holy Tradition. Holy Tradition teaches us how to live as Christians in the same way the apostles lived as Christians.

So, how do we know what to do in the Church? (Answer: "Holy Tradition!") How do we know how to worship God? (Holy Tradition!) How do we know what to believe about God? (Holy Tradition!) How do we know how to pray to God? (Holy Tradition!) How do we know how to live in a way that glorifies God? (Holy Tradition!) How do we know how to open ourselves to the grace of God? (Holy Tradition!) Yes! The answer is . . . Holy Tradition!

Have you ever gotten a present for Christmas that you really loved, but it came in a whole bunch of little parts you had to put together? Maybe a Lego set? Did you ever think, "How in the world am I going to put all this together?" How did you figure it out? Well, hopefully your gift came with instructions. The instructions explain about each part, what it looks like and what it's for, and how to put it together with other parts to build the set, right? The instructions aren't just words either. They have pictures and arrows and all kinds of helpful signs and symbols.

Holy Tradition is like the instructions for your Christmas present. Our Church Tradition provides us with instructions on how to live as a Christian and how the Church should function, so that we know God's truth and grace are flowing into us. Not everything we need to know is written down in one place. We have the Divine Liturgy and other Church services, and we have prayer books. We have the Church Councils and the Nicene Creed. We have the lives of saints that show us how to live a life in Christ. We have Church hymns that

teach us. There are pictures too in Holy Tradition: Icons. Sometimes we just see Holy Tradition by noticing how things are done in the Church and by listening to sermons, prayers, and hymns.

The river of Holy Tradition has several *smaller* streams that always come together as one big river. Let's talk about the five smaller streams in the one river of tradition.

1) First, we have the Divine Liturgy, Holy Communion, and all the Sacraments or Mysteries of the Church. Our Lord Jesus Christ instructed the apostles and showed them how the Church should serve the Liturgy, the Lord's Supper. He took bread and said, "This is My Body" (Matt. 26:26), and He took the cup of wine and said, "This is My blood" (Matt. 26:28). The apostles took the Divine Liturgy and all the grace-filled Holy Mysteries throughout the world wherever they preached and established churches. The Liturgy was done the same way throughout the world, even before the writing of the New Testament began. The Divine Liturgy, the Mysteries of Holy Baptism, Chrismation, Eucharist, Confession, Ordination, Marriage, Anointing for Healing (Unction), and all the services, prayers, and hymns of the Church are the first stream of Holy Tradition.

2) Next, we have the Holy Bible, or Scriptures. The Holy Bible has different writings from those who knew God, especially the prophets and apostles. This is the most important *written* part of Holy Tradition. It is called the written Word of God. The saints say the Bible is like a treasure chest full of precious and beautiful gems. The words of the Gospels are the words of our Lord Jesus. This is why we stand when we listen to the Holy Gospel during church services. The Holy Bible teaches us so much about how to live as a Christian and a member of the Church. But we need the rest of Holy Tradition too in order to understand the Bible.

3) The third stream of Holy Tradition is the Seven Ecumenical Councils. These are gatherings of the holy bishops from around the world. They teach us the truth about Jesus Christ and the Holy Trinity and guide us in living the true Faith. The Creed that we confess at baptism and in the Liturgy, the Nicene Creed, came from the first and second ecumenical Councils. The Councils also produced *canons*. The canons are like medical prescriptions or directions for good spiritual health. These teachings and canons help keep us from falling into dangerous spiritual waters.

4) Then there is the stream of the lives of the saints and their writings. The saints show us how to love God with all our heart, soul, mind, and strength. The writings of the saints, or Holy Fathers, are full of true teachings and instructions that make us strong and healthy Christians. They teach us the true meaning of the Liturgy, of the Holy Scriptures, and how to live a godly life.

5) Finally, we have the Holy Icons, the Church building (architecture), and Church music (hymnography). These communicate God's holiness to our eyes and ears . . . and through them to our hearts. They direct and tune our hearts to live in God's Kingdom.

These five holy streams make one great and deep river of tradition. And if we love God, we need to jump into the river of tradition. We need to swim in the *whole* river. We never just pick one or two streams and forget the rest. No! We take them all together. Together they form the river of grace called Holy Tradition.

Holy Tradition is like a mosaic. Do you know what a mosaic is? It is a picture made up of many small, colorful stones. Together all the parts of Holy Tradition form a beautiful and complete picture of Jesus Christ. And to see Christ is the greatest medicine of all.

Now, what are we to do with the Holy Tradition that has been passed down to us? What will you do with the Holy Tradition of the Church? Live it! Love it! and Lend it! Pass it down to others! When we do this, we become part of the river of grace of Holy Tradition when we practice it, protect it, and pass it down.

The Priesthood

Holy Tradition is like a river of grace that flows through the Church throughout the whole world. And we can drink of the wonderful waters of grace by living a spiritual life in the Church and following the holy teachings of our Faith. When we do that—when we really respect Holy Tradition and try to dive deeply into its waters—we can receive a lot of grace!

Remember that grace is God's own life. It's what keeps us spiritually healthy and holy. The river of grace is available to all of us, but God has given certain men a special responsibility to protect this river and to keep it clean and pure.

Have you ever seen a river or a lake that is dirty or polluted? You may have even smelled a river that has become contaminated because people have put things into the water that don't belong there, like trash or toxic chemicals. Can you drink water like that? And what happens if a lot of oil is spilled in a lake or river, or even an ocean? What happens to the fish or the frogs that live in the water, or the animals that drink from it? They get sick or they die, right?

From the time of the apostles some people have also tried to pollute God's river of grace by adding things to it that are not according to the teachings of the apostles. But even though some try to pollute the Holy Tradition, God promises to keep it clean. Jesus promised that the Holy Spirit would guide His Church

(John 16:13) and that evil would not be able to overcome or pollute the Church's Holy Tradition (Matt. 16:18).

Do you know why it is so very important to keep the Church's river of grace pure and clean? What will happen if we are not able to drink of God's pure grace? We will be in danger of losing the true Christian way of life and becoming spiritually ill. We might be separated from God, from His love and His life.

GUARDIANS OF GRACE

God has given to the Church special protectors to guard the river of grace and keep it from getting polluted. They guard the holy teachings of the Church. They also guard the holy things of the Church. Do you know who these guards are? The first guardians were the apostles, who were selected by Jesus. But who became the protectors of Holy Tradition after the apostles? It was the bishops and priests of the Church! And it is the same today.

Bishops and priests were ordained by the apostles to keep the river of grace flowing with holiness so we can drink of its waters and swim in it safely to God. Have you been to a swimming pool where you live? Are there certain things you shouldn't do at the pool because they are dangerous? What are some of those things? Running, diving in the shallow end, playing too rough, going into the deep end if you don't know how to swim well.

Or maybe you swim in a lake or in the ocean. Are there dangers in the ocean? What about really big waves or even sharks? Would you want to run into a shark?

Are there people at the pool or the ocean whose job it is to keep the swimmers safe, to keep them from getting hurt or drowning? Who are they? Yes, we call them lifeguards.

The bishops are like the head lifeguards of the Church. Their job is to protect God's people from drowning spiritually in the waves of sin and protect them from spiritual sharks who might hurt them with false teachings about God or His Church. So, with God's help the bishops are called to preserve the true Faith that Jesus gave to His apostles. And the bishops also ordain priests to be lifeguards in every church because the bishop himself cannot be in every place at the same time.

Now what is special about the bishops and priests? Are they really any different than anyone else? Are they only special because they wear unusual clothing? Is there something else that makes them special? Yes! And it is something very special indeed because it comes from God Himself!

What is it? It is called the gift or grace of the priesthood. A gift is something you receive from someone else, right? First it belongs to the one who is giving the gift. Then it becomes the property of the one who receives the gift. This gift of the priesthood is given to men who are called by God. The One who gives the grace of the priesthood is Jesus Christ, because the gift of priesthood comes from Him and belongs to Him. When He became Man, He became our High Priest, as the Bible tells us (Heb. 3:1; 4:14).

Now, this is a new and perfect priesthood. The Old Testament priests offered animals to God, asking Him for forgiveness of sins. They had to do this over and over again because they were not sinless and their offerings were not perfect.

But Jesus, the perfect priest, is sinless and made the perfect offering. He offered *Himself* to God His Father so that our sins and the sins of the whole world could be forgiven, "once for all" (Rom. 6:10; Heb. 7:27).

Jesus, our High Priest, overcame the devil and death by His own death and rose from the dead. And now He shares *His* perfect priesthood with His Church. In the Church, Jesus gives the gift of His priesthood to men whom He calls to guard the Church's river of grace. These are the bishops and priests of the Church.

So why are they special? They are special because in the Church, Christ lets them borrow *His* perfect priesthood. They don't become priests by their own power, but by *His* power. And they don't have their *own* priesthood, but Jesus' priesthood! And that is as special as it gets!

But how can a man receive the gift of Christ's perfect priesthood?

Do you remember in the Divine Liturgy—the priest calls down the Holy Spirit on the bread and the wine and they become something much more than bread and wine? They become the Body and Blood of Christ, right?

Something similar happens to make a man a priest. The Church calls the Holy Spirit down to make a man something more than he was before. The Holy Spirit makes a change in him, and God's grace makes him a priest, an icon of Christ, the High Priest.

Something special happens to this man when the Holy Spirit comes upon him. He has been *ordained*. He has received the Sacrament, or Mystery, of Holy Orders. He is no longer just "John," he is now "*Father* John," the "*Priest* John," a "priest of the Most High God" (Gen. 14:18; Heb.7:1). This is a great miracle! Because with Christ's grace, this *new* man is now able to call down the Holy Spirit upon the bread and wine at the Divine Liturgy. And through the priest's hand all the faithful Christians receive the Body and Blood of Christ.

The priest stands at the holy altar representing Jesus the High Priest. His hands become the hands of Jesus and his voice the voice of Jesus. Do you understand the miracle? Through the priest, heaven comes down to earth, just as God's Son, Jesus, came down from heaven, was born of the Theotokos by the Holy Spirit, and became Man.

Do you see what a great gift God has given to His Church? Can you imagine if there were no priests? Think about all the things the priest does because he has been given the priesthood of Christ. If there were no priests, there would be no Church!

It is through the priest that a person is baptized and born into eternal life. How important is that? Well, Jesus taught us that "unless one is born of water and the Spirit, he cannot enter the kingdom of God" (John 3:5). Pretty important!

Also, because of his ordination, the priest has the grace to anoint the newly baptized person with the holy chrism, the "seal of the gift of the Holy Spirit." The Bible says that "no one can say that Jesus is Lord except by the Holy Spirit" (1 Cor. 12:3). That's pretty important too!

Without the priest there would be no Divine Liturgy, no Holy Communion. That means no one could have the life of God living in their body and soul by eating and drinking the Body and Blood of Christ. Our Lord Jesus says, "unless you eat the flesh of the Son of Man and drink His blood, you have no life in you" (John 6:53). That's *really* important!

The priest is so important that one of the saints told us, "If you see a priest and an angel walking down the street, you must *first* go to the priest and kiss his hand before greeting the angel."[10] No angel has ever changed bread and wine into the Body and Blood of Jesus, but the priest does every time He serves the Divine Liturgy by calling upon the Holy Spirit! So, St. John Chrysostom says the priest is even higher than the angels.[11]

Because of this—because the priest reflects Christ and His priesthood—we should treat him with great love and respect, even though he is a human being and a sinner. Since he is an icon of Christ, we receive a blessing and kiss his hand when we see him. Because he brings God's grace to us, we honor him, we pray for him and are thankful for him. We do this because of Christ, who is with the priest in a special way since the time of his ordination. When we respect the priest, we show respect for Christ, for His Holy Church, and for the Holy Spirit who ordained him.

Do you know the three major orders of the priesthood? From the time of the apostles the Church has had three ranks of ordination within the priesthood of Christ: 1) bishop, 2) priest, or "presbyter," and 3) deacon. What is the difference between these three ranks?

First, there is the bishop. He is the leader among the priests and is called an "overseer" (Acts 20:28). Only he can ordain more priests or, with other bishops, make more bishops. He is like a shepherd who is in charge of the whole flock of Christ. We are Christ's sheep. The bishop protects us from "wolves" who might endanger us spiritually with false teachings. He is to teach the Faith, not according to his own ideas, but according to the Holy Tradition of the Church. The bishop receives this gift from Christ, who is called the "Shepherd and Overseer of your souls" (1 Pet. 2:25).

Next, we have the priests, or presbyters. These have the *same* priesthood as the bishop, but they are not overseers. They are not given the grace to ordain others. They serve at the holy altar and serve God's people with the blessing of the bishop. The priest has a small flock that is part of the larger flock of the bishop. He preaches, teaches, baptizes, serves the Divine Liturgy, performs marriages, and buries those who die. Along with the bishop, he is an icon of Christ since he sacrifices himself for God's people (John 10:11).

The third order is that of deacon. The word *deacon* means "servant." The first deacons (like St. Stephen, the first to be killed for Christ [Acts 7:59]) were ordained to help serve meals to needy Christians (Acts 6:2–3). Christ is the first "deacon" because He came to serve (Matt. 20:28). Deacons often serve the poor and help distribute Holy Communion to the sick. The deacon cannot serve the Divine Liturgy or other sacraments by himself, but he serves at the side of the bishop or priest, helping to bring God's grace to the people.

Through the bishops, priests, and deacons, the river of grace flows abundantly to all those in the Church, bringing refreshment to the hearts of Christians. And by their hands, new Christians are born through repentance and baptism, and they receive heavenly food, the Body and Blood of Christ.

Holy Communion

In the last lesson we learned about the guardians of grace—the bishops, priests, and deacons who help the river of grace to flow purely to all of us in the Church. Remember, this river flows down to us from Jesus and His apostles, and it is medicine for the illnesses of our souls. You and I are the man on the road in the Parable of the Good Samaritan, who need Christ to pour oil and wine onto our wounds and take us to the inn, the Church.

But it is not enough to know *about* our Church Tradition. It's not enough to know the Church has this river of grace. We have to dive into it. We need to swim in the river of grace. We need to drink from the river of grace so that God's power and life come into us, into our soul, into our heart, into our body and our blood. We have to *experience* the Holy Tradition.

Imagine sitting by a swimming pool on a very hot day, watching others swimming and enjoying the refreshing water. Maybe we don't have our swimming suit with us. So, we just sit and watch, getting more and more hot and uncomfortable. How nice it would be to feel the coolness of that water and to experience the joy we see on the faces of those who are swimming. How long will we wait without jumping in?

When we live and experience Holy Tradition, we will begin to understand what joy Christ has for us. He has made us to be His brothers and sisters, to enjoy His grace and to have God as our Father. When we swim in the waters of Holy Tradition, our hearts will become happy and full. God Himself will feed us and heal us in His Church. We will know God and His Kingdom!

"THE MEDICINE OF IMMORTALITY"

The most powerful way the river of grace flows to us in the Church is through the Divine Liturgy. Because in the Divine Liturgy, Jesus Christ—who became Man for us and shed His blood on the Cross for our sins and is risen from the dead—offers Himself to us again and again in His Body and Blood, so that, like Him, we might overcome death and live forever.

We call what happens in the Divine Liturgy "Holy Communion." Now, what does the word *communion* mean? Here's a hint: *commun*-ion and *commun*-ity share the same root word. A community is two or more persons sharing life together. Communion means living together in *union*, complete harmony, togetherness, and agreement.

The Divine Liturgy is Holy *Communion* because it is how the Church unites all people in Jesus Christ through His Body, the Church. We are united in the same Faith, the same baptism, the same Lord . . . the same Holy Tradition (Eph. 4:5). Everyone who unites themselves to Jesus Christ in the same Orthodox Faith and Holy Tradition is also in union—in *commun-ion*—with one another. So, in the

Church we have communion with Jesus *and* with one another if we agree with the Holy Tradition. When we receive Holy Communion together from the one loaf of bread and from the one chalice, we become one: one family, one community, one communion, one Church. We even become one with the perfect Community, the Holy Trinity—the Father, Son, and Holy Spirit!

Holy Communion unites us to God. When we receive Holy Communion with a pure heart, it becomes powerful medicine for our soul and body. One of the first bishops of the Church, who also died for Christ, St. Ignatius of Antioch, called Holy Communion "the *medicine* of immortality."[12]

We have learned that Jesus Christ is the medicine that heals us and brings us back to life with God. His Body and Blood is the strongest medicine of all and fills us with God's own life (John 6:54). As St. Ignatius said, it has the power to give us immortality. What is immortality? It means living forever with God and with God in us. Would you like to live like that forever? That can only happen if we are in communion with Jesus, if we are with Him and in harmony with Him and His Body.

Who served the very first Divine Liturgy? Do you know? It was Jesus Himself! Do you remember when He served the first Holy Communion? Sometimes it's called the "Last Supper," but we Orthodox Christians call it the "Mystical Supper," because it is a great Mystery by which Christ makes Himself known to us through eating and drinking.

Just before He gave himself to be crucified, on the same night He was going to be betrayed by his disciple, Judas, Jesus had a special meal with His disciples. It was a special meal that the Jewish people kept in order to remember God's blessings and to give thanks to Him.

But instead of saying the regular prayers, Jesus took the bread, blessed it, and gave it to His disciples and said, "Take, eat; this is My body" (Matt. 26:26). Then He took the cup of wine, gave thanks to God, and gave it to His disciples, saying, "Drink from it, all of you. For this is My blood of the new covenant, which is shed for many for the remission of sins" (Matt. 26:27–28).

Do you recognize these words? Yes, you should! We hear similar words each time we celebrate the Divine Liturgy. In the Divine Liturgy we remember how Christ offered His Body and Blood, both at the Supper and on the Cross. We not only "remember" it, we actually go there. We experience it! The Liturgy takes us back to that same Supper and to Christ's death and Resurrection.

Have you ever heard about the notion of time travel? That is the idea of being able to travel backward to an earlier time, or to be transported to a time in the future. The Divine Liturgy is a kind of spiritual time travel! God does not live within time, and His Kingdom is beyond time. There is no clock in heaven—it is always *now*! So, whenever we celebrate the Divine Liturgy, we return spiritually to be with Christ at the Mystical Supper, at the Cross and at the Resurrection. Each Divine Liturgy is the very same supper that Jesus had with His disciples.[13] Even though the priest says the words, it is always Jesus Himself who stands invisibly at the altar and offers His Body and Blood to us.

Holy Communion is so important that Jesus told us, "Unless you eat the flesh of the Son of Man and drink His blood, you have *no life* in you" (John 6:53). How terrible to be physically alive, but to have no *real* life! God forbid that we purposely stay away from Holy Communion, which gives us true life!

Have you heard of people giving blood to the Red Cross? Or have you heard about someone donating a kidney for someone whose kidneys were diseased or not working? By giving healthy blood or a healthy organ, we can save a sick person's body for a time. Jesus gives His Body and Blood to make us healthy spiritually and make our bodies immortal. Since He is risen from the dead and His Body is filled with eternal life, He gives us His Body to give us that same life. Since Jesus is God, God Himself lives within us when we receive Holy Communion.

Now, since we are receiving God into our souls and bodies, we are careful to prepare our hearts before receiving Holy Communion. Saint Paul tells us of some Christians who became sick because they didn't take care when receiving Christ's Body and Blood (1 Cor. 11:29–30).

How can we prepare for Holy Communion? First, we pray. We can go to Great Vespers on Saturday evening, since it helps to prepare our hearts. We can pray the special prayers (by ourselves or with our parents) that the saints left for us. If we are old enough, we may fast or go to Holy Confession to rid ourselves of sins in our hearts. But we don't just prepare the night before. We also prepare during the whole week by treating others with love and kindness, by showing love for God, and by being obedient to His commandments. All of these things open our hearts to receive Holy Communion in a way that makes the river of grace run right through our bodies and into our souls!

We also refer to the Divine Liturgy and Holy Communion as "the Eucharist." Do you know what this word means? *Eucharist* means "gratitude" or "thankfulness." So, every Divine Liturgy is a "thanksgiving," a giving thanks to God for our lives and for all His gifts. In the Divine Liturgy we thank God for all that He has given us, but especially for His greatest gift—for sending His Son, the Good Samaritan, to bring us back to life.

What are the "gifts" we offer to God in the Divine Liturgy? Bread and wine, right? Why bread and wine? Because they represent all the good things of this life—food and drink—that bring people life and joy. And what happens to bread and wine when we eat them? They become part of us. They become our own flesh and blood! So, the bread and wine also represent each of us who are made of flesh and blood. It's not only bread and wine that we offer to God on the altar, it is us too! We are offering *ourselves* to God! This is our gift to God.

And what does God do in return? What is His gift to us? He gives His own life to us in the Body and Blood of His Son, Jesus Christ. When we receive Holy Communion, His flesh and blood become our flesh and blood. There is no greater gift and no greater or stronger medicine!

Holy Baptism

In the last lesson we learned about the Divine Liturgy and Holy Communion. Holy Communion is the food and drink that makes us one with God and with one another.

Regular food and drink keep our bodies alive. Can our bodies live without eating? But the food and drink that God gives us to eat in the Church—Jesus' Body and Blood—doesn't just keep our bodies alive, it makes our souls live! Regular food fills our bellies, but Holy Communion fills us with the Holy Spirit—if we prepare our hearts with faith in God and love for Him, and we struggle to keep His commandments. Holy Communion gives us eternal life (John 6:54).

BORN INTO THE LIGHT

So, God has chosen to fill us with Himself through the act of eating. But what must happen before anyone can eat?

We have to wash our hands? Yes, but something else has to happen way before that.

We have to prepare our food? Yes, but there's something that comes way, way before that too!

We have to be hungry? Hmmm . . . Yes, we're getting warmer . . . but even way, way, way before that!

First, we have to be born, don't we? The same is true before we can eat the heavenly food of Holy Communion.

We have to be born again, not from our earthly mother, but from heaven. We need to be born into God's Kingdom. We have to be born from our mother, the Church, and become a child of God.

And how are we born in the Church? What is the Mystery that makes us into a new person, as if we are born again? (Here's a hint: When it happens, you should probably hold your breath. Another hint: We begin our new life with a splash!)

Did you get it? Yes, it is the Sacrament of Holy Baptism!

So, before we can be a member of the Church and be joined to Jesus' Body . . . before we can really drink from the river of grace in the Church . . . before we can taste the "Medicine of Immortality," Holy Communion, we have to be *born again* in Holy Baptism.

This is what our Lord said once to Nicodemus: "Unless one is born again, he cannot see the kingdom of God" (John 3:3).

Do you *see* how important Holy Baptism is?

Have you ever walked into a room that was dark and you didn't know where the light switch was? Did you put your hands out in front of you and start walking slowly and carefully?[T12] You may have been afraid you were going to trip or bump into something and hurt yourself, right? How nice it would be if someone could just turn on the light!

T12 A parent or teacher may demonstrate, closing one's eyes, or ask a child to demonstrate.

This is how our *soul* is before Holy Baptism. Our spiritual eyes are darkened, and we can't see Jesus, who is "the light of the world" (John 8:12). We walk, but we don't know where we're going (John 12:35; 1 John 2:11).

Did you know that another term for baptism is "Holy Illumination"? The saints teach us that when we are baptized in the Church we are illumined, or enlightened. Do you know what that means? It means we are lit up; the light goes on inside us, because Jesus the true light has come into us. If we have the light, then we can see where we are going and we can see the way to follow Jesus, to know the truth, to be healed, to do God's will, and to have true life. That's why Jesus said, "I am the way, the truth, and the life" (John 14:6).

Let's go back to the dark room for a minute. What happens if we can't find the light? We kind of get used to the darkness after a while, don't we? We learn to get around in the dark, and we may even forget what it's like to have the light. That's how it can be for some who don't know the light of Jesus, who don't have the Church, and who don't have Holy Baptism. We should always pray for them and for us, that we would truly find the light.

Do you remember the Good Samaritan? What did he do when he found the man who was half dead? Where did he take him? Yes, he took him to the inn, to the Church. God also asks us to bring others to the Church . . . and to always take ourselves as well! *Everyone* needs the light of Jesus Christ. And if we have it, we should try to share it with others by being an example of the light and by encouraging others to do so also.

Now, how do we baptize someone in the Church? Have you seen a baptism? It could be an adult, a baby, or an older child.

First, the priest prays to God (and we pray with him) that all the darkness of sin and of the devil would have no place in the one being baptized. We tell the devil to "get out of town!" And the priest asks the person (or the godparents if it is a little child) to reject the devil. He even asks them to spit on the devil!

Spitting on someone is not a nice thing to do, is it? We don't spit on people, because they are made in God's image. But we do spit on the devil, the evil one. If you spit on something, that means you don't want to have anything to do with it ever again!

Then the priest asks those who have come for baptism if they want to unite themselves to Jesus. This is very important! If we are going to be joined to Christ, we have to desire it; we have to really want it. If we are baptized as a small child, our godparents answer for us. But as we grow up, we have to make that same confession: "Yes, I unite myself to Christ!" Have you made that confession? Do you "believe in Him as King and God"?

Then to show exactly how and what they believe, the ones being baptized confess the Nicene Creed. You remember the Creed, right? The Creed expresses what we believe: "I believe in one God. . . ." Do you know the Nicene Creed by heart?

And what happens next? No, it's not quite time to baptize the person in the water. After praying for those who are about to be baptized, the priest says some long and important prayers asking the Lord to bless the waters of baptism. He asks that the Holy Spirit would come into the water so that those being baptized would become new and cleansed of all their sins. He asks that God would make the waters holy, just as Jesus did to the Jordan River when He was baptized. Imagine—the water in the baptismal font or river becomes just like the water of the Jordan after Jesus was baptized!

After this, those being baptized are anointed with the "oil of gladness." This is a sign that they are at peace with God and that God is about to give them great peace and joy in Holy Baptism.

And now they are baptized—in the name of the Father (*dunk*), and of the Son (*dunk*), and of the Holy Spirit (*dunk*). Do you know that the word *baptism* literally means "to dunk" or "to immerse" someone?

To be dunked under the water means that we are dying with Christ. And our coming up out of the water shows that we are being raised with Christ, who is risen from the dead (Rom. 6:4).

The saints tell us it is very important that we are dunked three times in the water. This shows our belief in the three Persons of the Holy Trinity. And it also shows that we believe in Jesus' three-day death, burial, and Resurrection.

After coming out of the waters, each person is given a new white robe. This is a sign that they have now been clothed with Christ. Do you remember the hymn we sing after the baptism? It comes from the Bible itself: "As many of you as have been baptized into Christ have put on Christ. Alleluia!" (Gal. 3:27). Do you know how to sing this hymn?

The white robe also shows that we have been for-given our sins and have been clothed in the light of Christ. (Remember that in Paradise, Adam and Eve were clothed in God's light!)

In Holy Baptism we become a new being. And so we receive a new name, a Christian name. If we are an infant, our parents may have already given us a Christian name. We are given a name that has been made holy by one of the saints of God, so that we can follow their example and ask for their prayers that we might become holy too.

And now we come to another very important moment.

Now that the "newly illumined" have put on Christ, they can also receive the Holy Spirit. And so, the priest takes very special oil, which is made and blessed by only certain bishops of the Church. It is called holy chrism—*chrism* means "gift." This is when the newly baptized receive the gift of the Holy Spirit. The priest anoints them as he says, "The seal of the gift of the Holy Spirit."

Now that they have been born into life with God in the Church, the priest leads them, with the Gospel Book in his hands, in a little walk or "dance"—a dance of joy around the baptismal font. This shows that their lives will be led by Christ and revolve around the life of Jesus and His Church.

And finally, those who have been born again are ready to eat and drink the Body and Blood of Jesus, so that Jesus is truly in their souls and bodies. Now that they are born from heaven, they begin to eat and drink the food of heaven.

This is Holy Baptism in the Holy Orthodox Church.

Repentance & Confession

So, now we know that our life in Christ begins at baptism. We become a new person, we become a member of the Church, and we are illumined—our hearts are lit up with God's light.

But then what? After we are baptized, do we take a vacation and forget all about it? No! Baptism is just the beginning of our Christian life. Remember, we said baptism is being *born* again.

The newly baptized person is just a little baby Orthodox Christian, even if they are eighty years old! We have to grow and become stronger in our faith, just like a baby has to grow and learn to walk and talk. We have to *keep* the faith with patience and endurance (Matt. 24:13; Rev. 14:12). The Bible tells us after we're baptized—after we receive the light—we need to continue to "walk in the light" (1 John 1:7). And if we do, the light of Christ in us grows and burns brighter and brighter.

WALKING IN THE LIGHT

Have you ever seen a campfire? What happens when you put more sticks or wood on it? The fire gets bigger, doesn't it? Or maybe you've seen your parents light a fire in a fireplace. Sometimes they blow just enough air on the fire to make it burn bigger and brighter.

This is like our spiritual life. When we are baptized, a fire is lit in our soul. It is the light of Jesus Christ. But if we want the fire to grow, we have to add more stuff to it, like adding sticks to a small fire. If we don't do anything, eventually the fire begins to go out. We need to add prayer and fasting, love and kindness, and more to our fire.

And most especially, we ask God to blow the Holy Spirit on that fire to make it burn hotter. We can do that by going to the church services with our fellow Orthodox Christians, where the Holy Spirit especially blows strong. And if we receive Holy Communion with faith and love, it makes the light of Christ in us grow.

But a fire is not always easy to keep going. What happens if we forget about the fire for a long time? It starts to die, doesn't it? Or what if a really strong wind comes and blows on the fire? It can blow it right out! And what if we pour water on the fire? That really puts our fire out quickly, doesn't it?

What is it called when we put out the fire in our soul, or keep it from burning brightly? It is called *sin*. Do you know what sin is? Are there things we may do that darken the light, that make the light of Christ smaller? Yes, and these are sins.

What is sin? It's doing bad stuff, right? But why are those things bad? The answer is that these things reduce the fire of Christ's love in our hearts. These things make our hearts cold. What happens when the campfire goes out but we're still outside? We get cold, don't we? That's like what sin does to us.

Now, have you ever seen someone shoot an arrow from a bow? Or maybe you've heard the story of Robin Hood. What is the sport called where people shoot an arrow at a target? Yes, archery! Did you know that the word for "sin" in the Greek language is an archery word? The word is *amarti'a*. Can you say it?—Ah-mahr-tee'-ah. It means "to miss the target."

When an archer hits the target, it means his aim is good and he is shooting straight. But when he misses the target, there's something wrong. His aim is off. The same is true for our soul. When we walk in the light of Christ, we are pointing ourselves toward God. We are hitting the target. But when we sin, we are shooting in the wrong direction. We have missed the target of what God created us to be and to do.

Is there anyone who hasn't missed the target? You, maybe? No, not really. We have all sinned. Adam and Eve were the first to sin, right? We say that they "fell" because they went from Paradise down into a world of sin. Remember the man who went *down* from Jerusalem to Jericho? Like him and like Adam, we fall too. It may only be that we fall in our mind, in our thoughts. But this is where every sin begins, in our thoughts. So we must be very careful to notice bad or strange thoughts and then dismiss them: brush them off like a fly that lands on our nose.

What do we do when we're playing and we fall down? Do we just stay there? No! We get back up, right? That's what we need to do when we sin too. And what do we call getting back up after we sin? It's called *repentance*. In Greek, the word is *metánia*. It means to change our focus and turn back to God. When we repent, when we think and do what is right, we bring light back into our nous, the eye of our soul. The holy Apostle Paul tells us that if we desire to live in Christ we "should repent, turn to God, and do works worthy of *repentance*" (Acts 26:20).

Sin darkens our baptismal light, but repentance brings the light of Christ back to our soul. Repentance means to turn away from sin, turn back to God, and walk back into His light. Have you ever gone too far from your house and weren't sure how to get back? Repentance is like coming back home.

Jesus told us the parable of the Prodigal Son (Luke 15:11–32). Do you know that story? A young man left his father and his home, and he went away to a country far away. But things didn't go well. He spent all his money, and he became lonely and hungry. But he remembered his father's love and his father's beautiful house, and he came to his senses. He realized he needed to go home. He began walking home to ask his father's forgiveness. Did his father forgive him? Yes! His father ran to greet him even before he made it all the way home! He embraced him, and kissed him, and forgave him. He even had a party for him because he was so glad he came home!

This is how God is with us when we repent and come back home. God is our Father, and the Church is our home. We should never be afraid to come back home if we sin.

In order to help us find our way home when we sin, the Church gives us a special way to say "I'm sorry" to God and to others. Do you know what this is called? It is called *confession* or the Sacrament of Repentance.

When we were baptized, we received our white baptismal robe. The robe meant that our soul had been washed clean. When we sin, we get our baptismal robe dingy and dirty. But a heartfelt confession makes it white and bright again.

Also, when we sin, we hurt our soul, and we need medicine to be healed. We come to confession to show Jesus our sin. And Jesus, our Physician, our loving doctor, heals us. The priest is Jesus' assistant, His helper. Jesus has blessed the priest to receive our confession and to help give our soul the Lord's medicine (John 20:21–23).

Is it sometimes scary when you have to go to the doctor? You might be afraid he's going to give you a shot or do something else that might hurt. But the medicine makes you feel better. Confession might seem scary sometimes too, but when we confess our sins, we feel better. Sin makes our soul sick. But repentance and confession keep us healthy. That's why it is good for us to confess our sins often. We want to keep our soul healthy and alive, and keep our hearts pure so we can truly see God in everything! (Matt. 5:8).

Repentance makes us clean again. Confession is like another baptism, but without water—except maybe the water of our tears (Matt. 5:4). When you get your body dirty, what do you do? You take a bath, right? Confession is like a bath for our soul. It has been called a "second baptism."

When the priest puts the stole over our head after we have confessed and says the prayer of absolution, it is like we are being baptized again, because we are being cleansed of our sins and the grace of God is being poured out upon us.

God is so good to give us the opportunity for confession, isn't He? And to give us a priest to help us with our sins, to point us back home. When we have confessed our sins, the priest places his stole over our head to show that God is covering our sins with His love, and then he prays for God's forgiveness for us.

God gives us repentance to fill us again with His light—to make our baptismal robe white. It's something we can work on every day. We can repent a little more each day.

But God never wants us to despair! Do you know what despair means? It means to lose hope, to think your sin can't be forgiven by repentance and the Sacrament of Confession. God is bigger and stronger than our sins. *Never* despair! Never be afraid to come to our loving doctor, Jesus Christ, to become healthy and clean again. Never be too ashamed or afraid to come home!

LESSON ELEVEN

Prayer

In the last lesson we learned how repentance is our path back to God. When we lose our way or wander off from home, repentance is what brings us back to God our Father and to our mother, the Church. And when we have made our hearts dark and dirty with sins, repentance and the Mystery of Confession allows us to get rid of the trash that has piled up in our heart, taking out the trash, cleansing our heart, and making room for the light and grace of Jesus to come back in.

But why do we need repentance? Shouldn't it be easy to love God and to follow His commandments? No, it is not easy! Why? There is one big reason: Because we forget! We forget God. This is the biggest problem we have as God's creatures and as Orthodox Christians.

REMEMBERING OUR BEST FRIEND

When Adam and Eve were in Paradise, God was their best friend. They never forgot Him. Not a day, not an hour, not a minute, not a second went by when they didn't feel their Friend with them. They didn't need to *try* to remember God, because their hearts were always with Him. Their hearts were praying to God all the time.

With every beat of their hearts, they remembered God and knew He was with them. And with every breath they breathed in God's love and goodness. Do you have to remember to breathe? Of course not! For Adam and Eve in Paradise, prayer was just like breathing.

But when they sinned, all of this changed. God did not change; *they* changed. God still loved them completely, but they could not feel his love like they used to. Their hearts became dull and darkened, and they didn't realize anymore that God was with them.

So, after a while they started making other "friends" that were not really friends at all, and they forgot God. Instead of remembering God, they thought of other things. What do you think some of those things were? How many possessions or how much money they could get? Why others seemed to have more than they did? How much food they could eat? How they could be better and more important or popular than their neighbor? They tried to make their hearts happy with things like these, but do you think it worked? No, it didn't. Not for long! Their hearts always ended up feeling empty. It is lonely to be without God.

Are these things really friends? They are not really friends, and certainly not *best* friends.

Now, do you have a best friend, or at least a very good friend? Do you love being with them? Do you think about them when you're not with them? Are you excited about the next time you will get to be with them? Do you feel somehow your hearts are joined together?

This is how we ought to be with God—like best friends. Do you forget your best friend? No! And we should try not to forget God either.

Do you know what it is called when we remember God? It is called *prayer*. Prayer is when our hearts are joined together with God. Prayer is not just talking or using words. When you're with your best friend, are you talking all the time? No! It is enough to be together! Prayer is being together with God. It is enjoying His friendship, His company. Prayer is what we do when we really love God—we *remember* Him.

Do you love God?

Once, St. Herman of Alaska was traveling on a ship. He began talking to the sailors who worked on that ship. He asked them about their lives and their families, their hopes and dreams. Then he asked them if they loved God. They said, "Of course we love God. Doesn't everyone? We go to church when we can. We try to do good to our neighbor."

Then St. Herman said, "I wish I truly loved God with all my heart. If I did, I would think of God at every moment. I would never forget Him. I would rejoice whenever I had time to be with Him. I would thank Him for all the good things in my life and even for the difficult things. I would always feel Him in my heart and all around me." Saint Herman was teaching them what it means to have true prayer.

The sailors looked around at each other. They realized maybe they didn't love God as much as they thought they did. Perhaps God was not really their best friend!

And St. Herman said, "From this day forward, from this hour, from this moment on, let us love God above all!" Prayer is what we do when we love God above all.

Now this kind of prayer doesn't come without some effort on our part. We don't start right away with this kind of prayer. We work up to it. We start at the beginning. We practice, practice, and practice again.

It may sound strange, but sometimes we even have to *force* ourselves to pray! Sometimes we may feel that we don't want to pray. But there are *many* things we don't want to do—for example: clean our room, mow the lawn, or apologize when we do something wrong. But after we do these things, we feel the reward of our effort. In the same way, when we practice prayer, we feel the blessing it brings.

So how do we learn to pray? Think about it. How did we learn to talk when we were just babies? Did we learn to talk with our mouth first or with our ears? Actually, it was with our *ears*. Our parents talked to us, and we listened. We listened to our brothers or sisters too if we had them. Slowly we started to use words too, right? We said "mommy," "doggy," "blankey." Then we began to speak in sentences. "Mommy, I'm hungry!"

So, we learned how to talk by listening to our mother. We learn how to pray also by listening to our mother, the Church. (And the Church has learned how to pray by listening to the Holy Spirit.) We learn how to speak to God by hearing the prayers of the Church. Many of those words come from the Bible. Our mother, the Church, shows us how to be with God as our best friend and to connect to Him in our hearts. She helps us know what words to use so our hearts can draw near to Him.

Our Lord, Jesus Christ, taught us how to pray to God as Father. God is Jesus' Father. But if we are united with Jesus in baptism and have been anointed with the same Spirit as Jesus in chrismation, we become like Jesus—a *son* of God (Gal. 3:26). Jesus is God's only *natural* Son. He has always been God's Son. But now, through Jesus Christ, we have become adopted into God's family as sons and daughters (Eph. 1:5). This means we now have Jesus as our brother and God as our Father. And so, Jesus gave us this most important prayer: "Our *Father...*" (Matt. 6:9–13). This prayer shows us how to pray as one of God's own beloved children.

If we want to connect with God, we must know Him as He is—as our Father and the Father of our Lord Jesus Christ. What we say to Him is very important. Now, remember your best friends here on earth. We should be able to speak freely with them. But can you say just anything to them? What if you say "I don't like you!" or "You're not fun!"? Do you think your friend would want to be with you if you said these things? Probably not. Certain things we say will bring us closer together while other things may be harmful to our relationship. For instance, if we lie to our friend, we may push our friend away and harm our friendship.

How we pray to God, how we address Him, the words we use are important! Our words have to be holy and humble and true. What if you said to your best friend, "You're ten feet tall!" or "You have three noses!"? It might be funny at first, but after a while your friend would feel like you don't really know them or appreciate them for who they are. Our words to God should be truthful.

God has given words of prayer to the Church through the Holy Bible, the Liturgy, the saints, and sometimes even the angels.

One of the most important prayers and hymns of our Church was taught to an Orthodox Christian boy by angels. Do you know which prayer? Do you know the story?

About 1,500 years ago, the great Christian city of Constantinople was being shaken by earthquakes. Not just one earthquake, but many earthquakes over a period of days and weeks. Some buildings were collapsing, and the people were afraid. Patriarch Proclus told the people to go outside of the city and pray. The whole city lived in tents outside of Constantinople and prayed together throughout each day, being led by the patriarch and priests.

Once, when the people were praying, a young boy was taken up from the crowd into heaven. His family thought a strong wind had swept him away, and they were sad. After a few minutes the boy came back down to his family. They were so happy to see him safe!

But something was different. The boy said he had seen angels and received from them a new prayer, which is sung in heaven. The angels told him to teach this new song to the patriarch and to all the Christians. And that is what happened.

As the boy sang the angel's song over and over to the patriarch, the people began gathering around to hear the new prayer given from above. Soon the patriarch also began to sing. One by one more voices were added—men, women, and children, all praying to God with this hymn until the sound seemed to fill the whole universe: "Holy God, Holy Mighty, Holy Immortal, have mercy on us!"

As quickly as the earthquakes had begun, now they stopped and did not return.

The prayers of the Church are not just any prayers. They are inspired by God and have the power to make holy those who pray them with faith. The prayers of the Church, our mother, are full of truth and grace, and through them we learn to pray in a way that unites us with God through Jesus Christ and the Holy Spirit.

The Church, our mother, not only teaches us how to pray, but she also instructs us to pray certain prayers at certain times each day. This is called a "prayer rule," because we use the same prayers at the same time every day. Orthodox Christians are to keep their prayer rule every morning and every evening, standing before the icons in their home. The morning is an important time to pray because we need to begin each day with God's presence and blessing. The evening is also a special time to thank God for the day that is past and ask for His protection and grace through the night. These two times of prayer are like our spiritual "bookends." They hold us together throughout the day and keep us strong, stable, and upright.

But as Orthodox Christians we don't just pray when we go to church, and we don't just pray in the morning and in the evening. We try to pray in our hearts all the time like Adam and Eve in Paradise.

The Church gives us another very important prayer to help us remember Christ at all times. It is one of the most important prayers of the Church and also one of the simplest. It is called the "Jesus Prayer."

Have you heard of the Jesus Prayer? "Lord Jesus Christ, Son of God, have mercy on me." Can you memorize this prayer? This simple prayer can be with us at any time—at home, at school, in church, when we're playing, when we're alone, when we're with friends.

Saying the Jesus Prayer is like walking through a field in the same place every day. What happens if you walk over weeds and brush over and over? You clear a path, a road, right? If we use the Jesus Prayer a lot, we make a path in our heart that keeps us always with God.

And this is the goal of prayer: To always be with God, our Best Friend.

LESSON TWELVE

Fasting

We have learned that real prayer is like being with our best friend. And truly God is our Best Friend, as He is closer to us than our own hearts.

When we spend time with our best friend, we use our mind to find words to speak, so we can talk and share with our friend. But do we only use our mind or our brain? When we are with our friend, do we only think and talk?

No, we use our body too, our whole body! We may use our hand to wave to our friend, or to ask them to come closer or to come quickly. We play games together and use our arms and legs. We might play hopscotch, run races, or play hide-and-seek. We may even hold hands or give our friend a hug.

We not only show our friendship with our mind and thoughts, but with our heart and our bodies as well. All of this helps us to know our friend and enjoy his or her company. What we do with our bodies helps us to share our lives with one another.

PRAYING WITH YOUR BODY

Now, the same is true when we spend time in prayer with our Lord. Yes, we speak with Him and to Him. We try to listen to Him also. But do we just use our minds to think or talk when we pray? What do the Holy Scriptures say about how we should love God? "You shall love the Lord your God with all your heart, with all your soul, with all your mind, and with all your strength" (Mark 12:30).

We love God and pray to Him with all that we are, and that includes our strength, our muscles, our bones, and every cell in our bodies. We can use our bodies to help our heart and our mind and our soul to pray, to be with God, and to know Him better.

When we spend time with our best friend, if we just sit around, we get bored and we lose interest in each other. Is that what *you* do when you're with your friends? Probably not, unless you broke your leg . . . or maybe both your legs!

Well, we don't usually just sit around when we pray to God either. If you haven't noticed already, we Orthodox Christians usually stand when we pray. Why? Because we're not bored, and we don't want our bodies to make us think we're bored. We stand because the holy God is standing with and before us.

Remember when Moses spoke with God in the burning bush? The Lord said to him, "Take your sandals off your feet, for the place where you stand is holy ground" (Ex. 3:5). In other words, "I (God) am present with you; you are in the presence of Someone greater than yourself. I need you to stand before Me and pay attention with reverence. We are going to spend time together!"

Do you think Moses bowed down to the ground when the Lord spoke? When we pray, we also bow before God to show our respect and love for Him. We make small bows (or *metánia*) and sometimes large bows called prostrations. Do you know how to make each of these bows?

When we use our bodies in this way, it helps remind our hearts and minds who God is—our Creator—and who we are—His creatures. We humble ourselves. The word *humble* comes from the word for *earth*. We bow down to the earth to remind ourselves that we are lower than God. We were created from the earth (Gen. 2:7; 1 Cor. 15:47). We put God in a higher place than ourselves.

We also bow down before and kiss holy icons, the holy Gospel Book, the holy Cross, and the bishop's and priest's hand to express our love and reverence for Christ.

What else do we do with our bodies when we pray? There is something we do all the time with our right hand and arm. Yes, we make the sign of the cross! We trace the cross over our bodies to bring the power and blessing of God into our mind (as we place our fingers to our forehead), our heart and soul (down to the belly), and our strength (from the right to the left shoulder).

And there is something else we do with our bodies in order to help us pray. We do it on Wednesdays and Fridays. We do it before Pascha and Christmas. We do it before the feasts of the Dormition of the Holy Theotokos and the Holy Apostles Peter and Paul. Did you get it yet? Yes, we *fast*!

What is fasting? *Fasting is forgetting about food in order to remember God.*

Fasting is turning our hunger for food into hunger for God. If we fast properly, it helps us to focus our mind and soul and heart on the Lord. When we fast, we empty our stomachs in order to fill our souls and hearts with prayer. The Lord Jesus told us, "Blessed *are* those who hunger and thirst for righteousness, for they shall be filled" (Matt. 5:6).

Fasting is prayer for our bodies. Because, as we said before, we are called to pray not just with our mind, but with our whole strength, with all our energy and focus, with our whole being, with our whole body. Fasting helps us to concentrate our energies on God and on doing His commandments.

The Holy Apostle Paul said this: Give your bodies as an offering to God, a living sacrifice, for this is acceptable worship (Rom. 12:1). In order to love God with our whole self, we fast from food or certain rich foods at certain times in order to give ourselves more fully to God. This is how our body prays to God together with our heart and mind.

Fasting also teaches us obedience.

Obedience means listening to God and to those God has placed in charge of us. Adam and Eve were not obedient to God in Paradise. God had asked them to fast from just one tree in the Garden. But they couldn't control themselves. They did not fast. They were disobedient.

Obedience is a very important virtue that can help lift us toward heaven. If we can obey, we can also love. Jesus said, "If you love Me, keep my commandments" (John 14:15).

Once St. Andrew, the holy Fool for Christ, saw a funeral procession. He saw two angels walking beside the coffin, one on each side. He asked them, "Who are you?" They answered, "We are the angels of the Wednesday and Friday fast. This man always fasted and prayed in obedience to God and His Church. By becoming obedient to God, he has become a lover of God, and now he can fly up to the God of love, into the Kingdom of heaven."

Do you like to fast? Do you *love* to fast?

Sometimes fasting doesn't seem very fun, does it? It's hard to be hungry. It's hard when our belly starts crying out to us, "Give me something to eat!" But if we turn our hearts to God at these moments, something very special can happen. We find that God can fill us with something more powerful than food.

Fasting is difficult at first, but if we practice patiently over and over again, we will notice ourselves gaining more and more strength inside. We will gain spiritual muscles. Does your dad or mom work out at the gym? What do they do? Lift weights, or run, or other kinds of exercise?

It's hard work, isn't it? When we exercise or run, we sweat, and our hearts beat harder and faster. Sometimes it makes us tired at first. But do we exercise to make ourselves weak? Of course not! Exercise makes us stronger. The more we exercise, the stronger we get. The more we run, the longer we can run, and the easier it gets.

Fasting is also like that. It's exercise for our spiritual muscles. It gives us endurance. That means we don't get tired as easily; we can pray more and not get tired.

Fasting gives us strength—strength to push away evil and strength to be obedient to God, strength to keep from hitting our brother or sister in anger, strength to be patient and kind when we don't feel like it, strength to think of others instead of ourselves, strength to stay calm when things go wrong, and strength to do the right thing when others around us are doing the wrong thing. Fasting helps us to say "no" to sin and "yes" to God. Fasting combined with prayer gives us great inner strength because God gives us His grace when we fast with hope and love.

Father Arseny was a rather small man and not very muscular. He had been put into a terrible prison in the Soviet Union because of his faith in Christ. The prisoners were given very little to eat. But unlike many others, Fr. Arseny not only fasted, but he prayed. Once a very large man in the prison, a criminal, was beating up a younger man. It looked as if he would kill him. Suddenly, small Fr. Arseny grabbed the arm of that large and muscular criminal and threw him across the room! Although Fr. Arseny did not have a powerful body, his prayer and fasting made him strong.

Fasting also makes our soul light and keeps us from being weighed down by sins. Saint Mary of Egypt fasted and prayed in the desert for forty-eight years. Her body became very skinny from eating so little food. But her fasting and prayer were like wings that lifted her up to God. Once, St. Zosimos saw her praying with her feet lifted completely off the ground! She had become like a spiritual bird, flying toward the the love of Christ on the wings of prayer and fasting. He also saw her walk on water, across the Jordan River.

Saint John Chrysostom said that fasting is one wing and prayer is the other. Have you ever seen a bird fly with one wing? With one wing the bird would spin in circles. We need *both* wings if we are to fly spiritually toward God.

Fasting helps us to pray, not just with our minds, but with our bodies too!

LESSON THIRTEEN
Almsgiving

Jesus has given us prayer and fasting to be like two wings, so we can fly to God. Fasting helps us to be strong and to learn how to control ourselves. If we can't fast from food, how will we fast from sin? If we can't control our stomach and our desires, how will we control our thoughts and our behavior?

Food is good. But too much food can make us slow and heavy, not just in body, but in soul. We fast in order to become light and free, free from bad desires and urges, free from sin. Our goal is to become holy or righteous, like God. We need to hunger not just for food, but for God and His righteousness. Jesus tells us, "Blessed *are* those who hunger and thirst for righteousness, for they shall be filled" (Matt. 5:6). Fasting helps our heart to hunger for God.

PRAYING WITH LOVE

Along with prayer and fasting there is a third thing we need. Without it, our wings will not be able to soar toward heaven. Do you know what it is? It is called "giving alms" or *almsgiving*. Jesus tells us about it in the Sermon on the Mount (Matt. 6:1–4).

What is almsgiving? What do we give when we give alms? Sometimes we give money, other times food. Sometimes we give someone a kind word or thoughtful gift. Other times we give our time, or we visit someone who is sick or lonely. Have you ever given alms?

Prayer and fasting are like two wings. But almsgiving is the "wind" that lifts our wings upward to God.

Have you ever had a kite? A kite can be a lot of fun, but if there is no wind, what happens? The kite won't fly; it falls to the ground. This is what happens when we pray and fast, but don't also give alms. Our prayers and our fasting may not fly up and reach God, because God is love. We could say that giving alms is like praying with love. Remember we said that fasting gives us strength? Well, almsgiving helps to turn our strength in the right direction. It turns our strength toward love. Remember the story of Cornelius, the Gentile who loved God? His prayers were heard by God because of his almsgiving (Acts 10:4).

And our God, the God of love, is always giving to us. He sends us rain; He gives us air to breathe; He gives us food and clothing. When we're sad, He often sends someone to cheer us up. He gives us parents and friends to love and care for us.

God gives us alms every day! Most importantly, God shows us mercy by forgiving our sins. God became Man, Jesus Christ, to show us mercy—to forgive us, to heal us, to embrace us so that we would never be alone. He died for us too, so we would not be alone even in death.

The word *alms* means "mercy." Do you know what mercy is? What does it mean to be merciful? Mercy means to care for others. It means we understand what a person is going through, and we want to help him. It means we care about other people's pain and suffering. We try to relieve their pain and give them comfort and hope . . . not just comfort for their body, but hope for their heart.

Our Lord Jesus said, "Blessed are the merciful" (Matt. 5:7). Why should we be merciful to others? Because God shows mercy to us. God is merciful! God always cares about us, our needs, our pain, our hopes and our fears, and He always tries to help us. Remember the Parable of the Good Samaritan? Who is the Good Samaritan? Who is it who had mercy on the man who fell among the robbers? Who showed compassion and love to Him? Who poured medicine on his wounds and took him to the inn? It was Jesus, our Good Samaritan.

Now, if God shows us mercy, we should show mercy to others, right? Jesus teaches us, "Blessed are the merciful." But He also tells us that if we are merciful, God will give us even more mercy. When we are merciful, God sends even more love and mercy into our hearts: "Blessed are the merciful, *for they shall obtain mercy*" (Matt. 5:7). Give mercy, get mercy!

Jesus tells us in the Sermon on the Mount that we need to give alms. But He tells us we need to do it in the right way. What is the right way? We have to do it for God and not to be seen by other people.

Jesus tells us to be careful not to give alms or to do good deeds in order to be seen by others. He says, "When you show mercy to another, don't blow a trumpet so that everyone will notice what you're doing" (Matt. 6:2). *Doo-doo-do-dooooo!!* "Look at me! I'm doing a good deed!"

Is a trumpet loud? Does a trumpet make people turn their heads and look at you? Yes! The Lord is telling us to do good so that *God* will notice, not other people. Because then God will reward us. If we do it so that others will think we are good or special, we may become prideful, and there is no heavenly reward in that.

Do you remember St. Nicholas? What did he do? How did he help the poor family? Didn't he *secretly* give them bags of gold?

So, if we give alms in secret—just because we love God and others—God will reward us. How will He reward us? With candy? Maybe with a new toy from Mom and Dad? No, not that kind of reward.

God rewards us in a very special way that lasts forever. Do candy or toys last forever? Every time we give alms and show mercy to those in need, with love for God, do you know what happens? Our hearts grow bigger! Our hearts get bigger because more of God's love comes into us. And when our hearts get bigger, we can pray better, and we can fast better. Then our hearts get even bigger! Pretty soon the whole world and all the people of the world can fit into our hearts because we love as God loves. If God can fit into our hearts, then everything else can too!

People with little, tiny hearts have a really hard time loving and showing mercy. But God wants our hearts to be really big. Is your heart big? Can it get bigger? Are you giving alms so that you will have rewards in heaven?

There is something even more amazing that happens when we give alms or mercy.

Every human being is made in God's image. That means Jesus Christ is in every person. And Jesus especially loves and cares about those who are suffering and in need. Jesus Himself suffered on the Cross, didn't He? If Jesus lives in those who suffer and are in need, and we give alms to those in need, who are we really giving to? To Jesus Himself!

Once, St. Martin was riding on his horse toward a city. He was a soldier and also a catechumen in the Church. He was only eighteen years old. He wasn't sure about being baptized. When he came to the gate of the city, he saw a beggar who was wearing rags for clothing. It was a very cold, snowy day.

Immediately, the catechumen Martin took his sword and cut his beautiful and expensive soldier's cloak in half and gave half of it to the beggar to keep him warm. That night he had a dream. Jesus appeared to him with a host of saints around Him. Jesus was wearing the cloak that St. Martin gave to the beggar! Then Jesus turned to the saints and said: "Look! This is the cloak that Martin, who is only a catechumen, gave to Me." After this, Martin went immediately to be baptized.

When we give food or drink to the needy, when we visit the sick, when we are kind to strangers, when we comfort those who are lonely or in prison, we are doing it to Jesus Himself!

This is what He teaches us: "Inasmuch as you did *it* to one of the least of these My brethren, you did *it* to Me" (Matt. 25:40).

When we pray, we show that we have *faith*. Faith is belief and trust in God. It is trusting that God is true and will take care of us, no matter what. It is a knowledge of things that we cannot see with our physical eyes (Heb. 11:1).

When we fast, we show our *hope* in God. We don't hope in the things of this world, but in God, who knows what we really need and who gives us what we really need. Our hope is in heaven (Col. 1:5).

When we give alms, we show that true faith and hope in God lead to *love* for God and for all God made. Almsgiving brings God's love and mercy into our lives and into the lives of others and all creation. When we show love and mercy, we imitate God, who loved us by sending His Son to have mercy on us (John 3:16).

Faith, *hope*, and *love* are the three great virtues of the Christian life (1 Cor. 13:13). Everything we have learned in our catechism is meant to lead us to these qualities and to this virtuous way of life, so that we may be united to our one God and Father, through His Son, our Lord and Savior, Jesus Christ, by the power and grace of the Holy Spirit—the Holy Trinity, one in essence and undivided.

Amen!

NOTES

LESSON I

1   Saint Euphrosynos the Cook is one example. According to his *Life*, a hieromonk living in the same monastery was allowed by God to see the saint in Paradise one night in a vision as he slept. The priest asked Euphrosynos if he might bring something back from Paradise to the monastery. The saint gave him three apples wrapped in a cloth. When the priest awoke he found the fragrant apples wrapped in the cloth at his bedside. Saint Euphrosynos admitted that he had been, by God's mercy, in Paradise the previous night.

2   Saint Seraphim of Sarov is very clear on this point. See his conversation with Motovilov.

3   "When trees and ripe fruit rot and fall to the ground they turn into sweet-scented soil, free from the smell of decay exuded by the vegetable matter of this world. That is because of the great richness and holiness of the grace ever abounding there" (St. Gregory of Sinai, *On Commandments and Doctrines*, 10).

4   "[Paradise] is temperate, and the air that surrounds it is the rarest and purest: evergreen plants are its pride, sweet fragrances abound, it is flooded with light, and in sensuous freshness and beauty it transcends imagination" (St. John of Damascus, *An Exact Exposition of the Orthodox Faith*, Book II, Chapter XI).

5   "Before the Fall men lived in Paradise like angels; they were not inflamed with lust, were not kindled by other passions either, were not burdened with bodily needs; but being created entirely incorruptible and immortal, they did not even need the covering of clothing" (St. John Chrysostom, *Homilies on Genesis* 13:4, 15:4).

6   "God then made man without evil, upright, virtuous, free from pain and care, glorified with every virtue, adorned with all that is good" (St. John of Damascus, *An Exact Exposition of the Orthodox Faith,* Book II, Chapter XII, Concerning Man).

7   Saint John of Damascus explains that paradise is twofold, both material and immaterial. "The divine Paradise is twofold. . . . The life in the soul is passed in a place far more sublime and of more surpassing beauty, where God makes His home, and where He wraps man about as with a glorious garment, and robes him in His grace, and delights and sustains him like an angel with the sweetest of all fruits, the contemplation of Himself" (*An Exact Exposition of the Orthodox Faith*, Book II, Chapter XI, Concerning Paradise). Saint Gregory of Sinai agrees and teaches the same (*Writings from the Philokalia*, p. 39).

LESSON 2

8 Saint John Chrysostom makes this point no less than ten times in his homilies 16–17 on Genesis.

LESSON 3

9 For example: "The body sees by means of the eyes, and the soul by means of the [nous]" (St. Anthony the Great, *Philokalia*, Vol. 1., p. 347). "When the soul's eye, the [nous], has been darkened by these three, the soul is dominated by all the other passions" (St. John of Damaskos, *Philokalia*, Vol. 2, p. 335).

LESSON 7

10 Although not an exact quote, this is attributed to St. Cosmas of Aitolia (+1779).

11 "What great honor the grace of the Spirit has vouchsafed to priests. . . . For they who inhabit the earth and make their abode are entrusted with the administration of things which are in Heaven, and have received an authority which God has not given to the angels or archangels" (*On the Priesthood*, 3).

LESSON 8

12 Epistle to the Ephesians, 20.

13 This is explicitly stated by St. John Chrysostom. See Hieromonk Gregorios, *The Divine Liturgy: A Commentary in the Light of the Fathers*, trans. Elizabeth Theokritoff (Columbia, MO: Newrome Press, 2009), 18.

ABOUT THE AUTHOR

V. REV. FR. MICHAEL SHANBOUR is an Orthodox Christian of sixty years, serving in the Antiochian Orthodox Christian Archdiocese. From his teen years he began reading church history and theology, often contemplating how the Orthodox Faith could be explained to non-Orthodox in America. He was active in youth, camp, music, and Christian education ministries. He received his Master of Divinity at St. Vladimir's Orthodox Theological Seminary in 1989, graduating *cum laude*. During that time, he was a founding member of the popular Orthodox music group, Kerygma, along with (now) Bishop Anthony Michaels and Fr. Patrick Kinder of blessed memory. Later, he served as Outreach Committee Chair for his home parish of St. George Cathedral in Wichita, Kansas, and as Youth Director for St. Mary Church in Livonia, Michigan (1995-97).

In 1997 he married Makrina Copeland from Yakima, Washington and moved to Omaha, Nebraska, where she attended medical school. He was ordained to the holy diaconate in 1998 and served at St. Mary Church in Omaha, where he composed and recorded the popular children's musical album, "Living in an Orthodox World." Ordained to the holy priesthood by Bishop Basil Essey in 2001, Fr. Michael

pastored mission parishes in Topeka, Kansas and Spokane, Washington before founding Three Hierarchs Church in Wenatchee, Washington in 2010.

Fr. Michael has taught online classes for St. Athanasius Academy, St. Raphael School, and the Classical Learning Resource Center (CLRC). His retreat, "The Way of Escape: Overcoming Temptation and Sin," is available on Ancient Faith Radio.

Alongside his teaching and outreach, Fr. Michael is the author of the best-selling Orthodox book, *Know the Faith: A Handbook for Orthodox Christians and Inquirers*, published in 2016 by Ancient Faith Publishing. In 2019 he self-published *The Good Samaritan: A Children's Catechism*, perhaps the first comprehensive youth catechism (ages 8-12) in the English language. Written to inform and inspire youth, the creation of the catechism is being used as a fundraiser to help the Three Hierarchs community's efforts to build a new church. Ancient Faith Publishing has since taken on the production of *The Good Samaritan* to ensure availability of this resource to the broader Orthodox Christian community.

Fr. Michael is blessed to live in Wenatchee, WA and share his life with his Khouria Makrina, and son, Simeon.

We hope you have enjoyed and benefited from this book. Your financial support makes it possible to continue our nonprofit ministry both in print and online. Because the proceeds from our book sales only partially cover the costs of operating *Ancient Faith Publishing* and *Ancient Faith Radio*, we greatly appreciate the generosity of our readers and listeners. Donations are tax deductible and can be made at
www.ancientfaith.com

ANCIENT FAITH
PUBLISHING

To view our other publications,
please visit our website:
store.ancientfaith.com

Bringing you Orthodox Christian music, readings, prayers, teaching, and podcasts 24 hours a day since 2004 at
www.ancientfaith.com